W9-BBF-925

MASTERMINDS Riddle Math *Series*

FRACTIONS, RATIO, PROBABILITY, AND STANDARD MEASUREMENT

Reproducible Skill Builders And Higher Order Thinking Activities Based On NCTM Standards

By Brenda Opie, Lory Jackson,
and Douglas McAvinn

Incentive Publications, Inc.
Nashville, Tennessee

Illustrated by Douglas McAvinn
Cover illustration by Douglas McAvinn

ISBN 0-86530-302-9

PRINTED IN THE UNITED STATES OF AMERICA

TABLE OF CONTENTS

INTRODUCING FRACTIONS
Where in the World? 1
The Case of the Numerator and Denominator 2

FINDING MULTIPLES AND LEAST COMMON MULTIPLES OF COMPOSITE NUMBERS
What happens to a thief if he falls into a cement mixer? (He becomes a hardened criminal) 3

FINDING COMMON AND GREATEST COMMON FACTORS OF COMPOSITE NUMBERS
Factors 4
What does the invisible man drink at snack time? (Evaporated Milk) 5
Who are the slowest talkers in the whole world? (Convicts - They spend 25 years on a single sentence) 6

LOCATING PRIMES, COMPOSITES, AND PRIME FACTORS
Sieve of Erathosthenes 7
Prime Search 8
Prime or Composite? 9
Factor Trees 10
Factor Trees 11
Prime Factorization 12

PUTTING IT ALL TOGETHER: (Multiples, factors, primes, composites, and prime factors)
Using the Slide 13
Antics 14

FINDING EQUIVALENT FRACTIONS
Chocolate Delight 15
Why didn't the skeleton cross the road? (Because it didn't have any guts) 16
What does a worm do in a corn field? (It goes in one ear and out the other) 17

SIMPLIFYING FRACTIONS (Reducing fractions to lowest terms)
Why did Humpty Dumpty have a great fall? (To make up for his miserable summer) 18
What did Mrs. Claus say to her husband during the rainstorm? (Come and look at the reindeer)..............19
Why did the umpire throw the chicken out of the game? (He suspected foul play).......................20

CONVERTING MIXED NUMERALS AND IMPROPER FRACTIONS
Ghoulish definitions...21
Daffy Definitions 22
Phobias! Phobias! Phobias! 23

COMPARING FRACTIONS
How many months have 28 days? (All of the months do). 24

ADDING AND SUBTRACTING LIKE FRACTIONS
What happens when the frog's car breaks down? (He gets toad away).................................25
Why did the astronaut take a shovel into space? (To dig a black hole).................................26

ADDING AND SUBTRACTING UNLIKE FRACTIONS
Why is six afraid of seven? (Because seven ate nine) 27

Why did the Cyclops have to close his school? (Because he had only one pupil) 28

What's the only thing to eat on a deserted island? (Only the sand which is there) 29

ADDING MIXED NUMERALS WITH NO REGROUPING

What is the nationality of Santa Claus? (He is North Polish) 30

ADDING AND SUBTRACTING MIXED NUMERALS WITH REGROUPING

Where is the only place in the world an elephant can visit the dentist? (Tuscaloosa, Alabama) 31

What is the coldest place in the theater? (In Z row) 32

What's grey, heavy, and sends people to sleep? (A hypnopotamus) 33

How do Martian cowboys greet each other? (With communication saddlelights) 34

What meal did the Revolutionists serve to catch spies? (Chicken catch a Tory) 35

What did one magnet say to the other magnet? (I find you very attractive) 36

SOLVING WORD PROBLEMS WITH ADDING AND SUBTRACTING FRACTIONS

What does an elf do after school? (Gnomework) 37

What do you get when you cross an Arabian ruler and a cow? (A milksheik) 38

MULTIPLYING FRACTIONS WITH _OF_

What did the cashier say when he was caught stealing? (I thought the change would do me good) 39

MULTIPLYING SIMPLE FRACTIONS

Tickle Your Funny Bone 40

Mathosaurus: Who Am I? 41

MULTIPLYING MIXED NUMERALS

Math Bingo 42

What's a lazy rooster? (A cock-a-doodle don't) 43

DIVIDING SIMPLE FRACTIONS

Why did the spy pull the sheets over his head? (He was an undercover agent) 44

Why is baseball like a pancake? (Because its success depends on the batter) 45

Why was the Egyptian girl worried? (Because her daddy was a mummy) 46

What's beautiful, grey and wears glass slippers? (Cinderelephant) 47

DIVIDING MIXED NUMERALS

Why is Dracula a great artist? (He can draw blood) 48

Trivia: Who Am I? 49

ADDING, SUBTRACTING, MULTIPLYING AND DIVIDING MIXED NUMERALS

Why was William Shakespeare able to write so well? (Where there's a Will, there's a way) 50

**SOLVING WORD PROBLEMS WITH ADDING, SUBTRACTING,
MULTIPLYING AND DIVIDING FRACTIONS**

What kind of music do ghosts like? (Spiritual music) 51

Mathosaurus: Who Am I? 52

USING STANDARD MEASUREMENTS: FEET, POUNDS, YEARS, AND TIME ZONES

Why was Cinderella thrown off the baseball team? (She ran away from the ball) 53

Dozens, Dozens, Dozens..54
How does a broom act? (With sweeping gestures) 55
How many kinds of gnus are there? (Only two: good gnus and bad gnus) 56
What insects were common in the time of King Arthur's Court? (Gnats of the Round Table) 57
Why is your nose in the middle of your face? (Because it's the scenter) 58
When do old clocks die? (When their time is up) 59
What did one candle say to the other? (Let's go out together) 60

USING RATIOS, RATES, AND PROPORTIONS
Which is more correct to say, 8 + 4 is 11 or 8 + 4 are 11? (Neither, 8 plus 4 is 12) 61
Ratio Survey 62
Why doesn't Sweden export cattle? (She wanted to keep her Stockholm) 63
Why didn't the skeleton kid want to go to school? (His heart was not in it) 64

EXPLORING PROBABILITY
Marbles and probability...65
Nickel Toss 66
What Are the Odds? 67-68
Rock, Paper, Scissors..69

BRAIN CHALLENGERS: FRACTIONS, RATIOS, AND PROBABILITY 70
Domino Fractions 71
Domino Fractions II 72
Combining Fractions 73
Number Maze 74
Number Maze II..75
Photo Album 76
Fraction Letter Code 77
Fraction Letter Code II 78
Fractional Parts 79
Fraction Box 80
Fraction Box II 81
Birthday Party 82
Symbol Fractions..83
Matching Ratios to Form Proportions 84
Using Ratios to Save Money 85
52 Card Probability..86

ANSWER KEY..87-91

Where in the world?

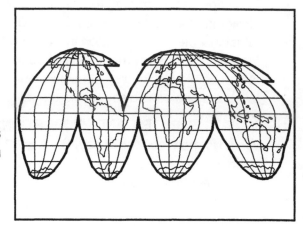

DIRECTIONS: Think of many, varied and unusual places or ways that fractions are used in our world other than in your math book. Try to think of at least 12.

1. _____

2. _____

3. _____

4. _____

5. _____

6. _____

7. _____

8. _____

9. _____

10. _____

11. _____

12. _____

13. _____

14. _____

15. _____

16. _____

EXTENSION ACTIVITY: Divide a sheet of paper into fourths. Choose four different ways fractions are used in our world and illustrate them. Write a phrase to explain each picture. You may want to add color to your illustrations.

THE CASE OF THE NUMERATOR AND DENOMINATOR

Directions: Numerators and denominators share a very special relationship that involves the understanding of how a part can relate to its whole. Think of many, varied and unusual pairs that have a similar relationship as a numerator and a a denominator. Examples are: checkers to a board, heart to a body, CDs to a CD player.

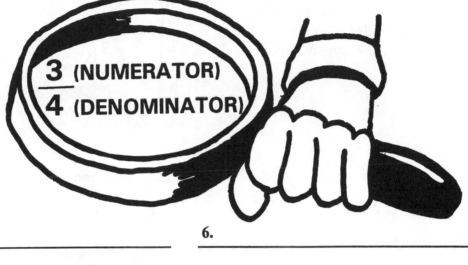

$\frac{3}{4}$ (NUMERATOR)
(DENOMINATOR)

1. _____

2. _____

3. _____

4. _____

5. _____

6. _____

7. _____

8. _____

9. _____

10. _____

EXTENSION ACTIVITIES: (1) Illustrate one or more of your relationships. (2) Imagine you have a friend who cannot remember the difference in a numerator and a denominator. Think about a clever way to help your classmate remember *which is which*. In the space provided below, describe your clever plan.

_____

_____

_____

3

NAME_____

WHAT HAPPENS TO A THIEF IF HE FALLS INTO A CEMENT MIXER?

DIRECTIONS: Figure out the *least common multiple (LCM)* for each pair of numbers. Each time this multiple occurs in the decoder, place the letter of the multiple in the appropriate space.

1. LCM of 3 and 5 = _____ M

2. LCM of 4 and 7 _____ L

3. LCM of 12 and 8 = _____ B

4. LCM of 15 and 9 =_____ E

5. LCM of 20 and 15 = ____ C

6. LCM of 11 and 33 = ____ N

7. LCM of 3 and 10 = _____ A

8. LCM of 12 and 18 = ____ R

9. LCM of 16 and 4 = ____ I

10. LCM of 16 and 12 = ____ H

11. LCM of 10 and 4 = ____ D

12. LCM of 6 and 9 = ____ S

13. LCM of 4 and 8 = ____ O

| 48 | 45 | 24 | 45 | 60 | 8 | 15 | 45 | 18 |

| 30 | 48 | 30 | 36 | 20 | 45 | 33 | 45 | 20 |

| 60 | 36 | 16 | 15 | 16 | 33 | 30 | 28 |

NAME _____

Factors

List all the factors of each of the composite numbers.

1. 18 _____

2. 16 _____

3. 24 _____

4. 30 _____

5. 12 _____

6. 32 _____

7. 60 _____

8. 35 _____

Find the greatest common factor for each group of numbers.

9. 24, 30 _____

10. 16, 18 _____

11. 12, 60 _____

12. 15, 30 _____

13. 12, 32 _____

14. 16, 30 _____

15. 16, 24 _____

16. 30, 60 _____

17. 12, 18 _____

18. 35, 60 _____

Add all of the greatest common factors and your total should be either 86, 90, 94, or 108.

Your final answer is _____ .

Finding factors of a composite number

WHAT DOES THE INVISIBLE MAN DRINK AT SNACKTIME?

NAME

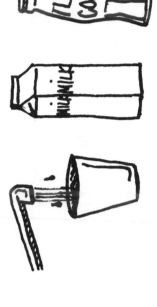

Directions: Find the missing factor in each set of numbers. Each time the factor appears in the decoder, write the letter above the appropriate space.

FACTORS OF 36:
{1, 2, 3, 4, 9, 12, 18, 36, A}
A =

FACTORS OF 32 :
{1, 2, 4, 8, 32 D}
D =

FACTORS OF 70 :
{1, 2, 5, 7, 10, 14, 70, I}
I =

FACTORS OF 72:
{1, 2, 3, 4, 6, 8, 12, 18, 24, 36, 72, K}
K =

FACTORS OF 48:
{1, 2, 3, 4, 6, 8, 12, 16, 48, V}
V =

FACTORS OF 12:
{1, 2, 3, 6, 12, E}
E =

FACTORS OF 16:
{1, 4, 8, 16, L}
L =

FACTORS OF 20:
{1, 2, 4, 10, 20, T}
T =

FACTORS OF 26 :
{1, 2, 26, R}
R =

FACTORS OF 15:
{3, 5, 15, M}
M =

FACTORS OF 60 :
{1, 2, 3, 4, 5, 6, 10,12, 20, 30, 60, P}
P =

FACTORS OF 22:
{1, 2, 22, O}
O =

4	24	6	15	11	13	6	5	4	16	1	35	2	9

Finding the greatest common factor

WHO ARE THE SLOWEST TALKERS IN THE WHOLE WORLD?

DIRECTIONS: Figure out the *greatest common factor (GCF)* for each pair of numbers. Each time the greatest common factor occurs in the decoder, place the letter of the GFC in the appropriate space.

1. GCF of 10 and 15 = ____ Y
2. GCF of 12 and 16 = ____ I
3. GCF of 50 and 75 = ____ R
4. GCF of 16 and 48 = ____ E
5. GCF of 50 and 100 = ____ D
6. GCF of 30 and 70 = ____ H
7. GCF of 17 and 34 = ____ A
8. GCF of 11 and 22 = ____ N
9. GCF of 15 and 60 = ____ S

10. GCF of 12 and 24 = ____ P
11. GCF of 6 and 8 = ____ G
12. GCF of 21 and 36 = ____ 2
13. GCF of 7 and 14 = ____ V
14. GCF of 6 and 12 = ____ 5
15. GCF of 24 and 72 = ____ L
16. GCF of 18 and 27 = ____ O
17. GCF of 24 and 64 = ____ T
18. GCF of 21 and 22 = ____ C

Decoder:

___ ___ ___ ___ ___ ___ ___
15   9   11   7   4   1   8

___ ___ ___ ___ ___ ___ ___ ___ ___
12   16   11   50   17   3   15   6   10

___ ___ ___ ___ ___ ___ ___ ___ ___ ___ ___
9   11   16   11   15   8   16   4   2   24   25

___ ___ ___ ___
15   16   1   16

Finding primes

SIEVE OF ERATOSTHENES

BACKGROUND INFORMATION: A *prime number* is a whole number that has exactly two factors, itself and 1. This means that 7 is a prime number, and 4 is not. Since 1 has only one factor, 1 is not a prime number. More than 2,000 years ago, a Greek mathematician, Eratosthenes, invented a system for finding prime numbers. This system is called the *Sieve of Eratosthenes.* It is based on a number grid.

DIRECTIONS: Use the grid system of numbers from 1 to 100 to locate those primes less than 100. First, cross out 1. Then, using a |, cross out all the multiples of 2. Using a —, cross out all the multiples of 3. Using a \, cross out the multiples of 5, and finally using /, cross out all the multiples of 7. *(It may be helpful to use different color crayons for each of the crossing out symbols.)* Those numbers that have no cross marks are primes.

1	2	3	4	5	6	7	8	9	10
11	12	13	14	15	16	17	18	19	20
21	22	23	24	25	26	27	28	29	30
31	32	33	34	35	36	37	38	39	40
41	42	43	44	45	46	47	48	49	50
51	52	53	54	55	56	57	58	59	60
61	62	63	64	65	66	67	68	69	70
71	72	73	74	75	76	77	78	79	80
81	82	83	84	85	86	87	88	89	90
91	92	93	94	95	96	97	98	99	100

List all of the 25 primes that are less than 100:_____

_____

_____

NAME_____

PRIME SEARCH

DIRECTIONS: Use the complete *Sieve of Eratosthenes* to answer these questions.

1. How many primes numbers are there less than 100?_____

2. How many even primes?_____List._____

3. How many primes begin with 9?_____List._____

4. Which column has the greatest number of primes?_____

5. How many columns have only one prime?_____List._____

6. How many primes begin with 8?_____List_____

7. Which rows have 4 primes? _____

8. How many columns have 5 primes?_____

9. Twin primes have only one natural number between them, such as 11 and 13. How many more twin primes are there on this chart?_____

   List the pairs =_____

10. Which row has the fewest primes?_____List._____

EXTENSION ACTIVITY: On a separate sheet of paper, make your own grid for the numbers 101 to 200. Find all the prime numbers. Is the total number of primes more, less, or equal to the number of primes from 1 to 100? Explain.

_____

9

Deciphering numbers as primes or composites

PRIME OR COMPOSITE?

Primes are numbers with exactly 2 factors. For example: 11 has only one set of factors, 11 and 1.

Composite are numbers with more than 2 factors. For example: 15 has 15 and 1, and also 3 and 5.

Directions: Complete the table below. If the number is a composite, you will need to give only one set of factors to prove that the number is not prime. (*For example, if the number is 24, you can give 6 and 4, or 12 and 2, or 8 and 3, but you need to only give one set.*)

	NUMBER	FACTORS	PRIME OR COMPOSITE?
1.	2	1,2	Prime
2.	3		
3.	4		
4.	5		
5.	6		
6.	7		
7.	8		
8.	9		
9.	10		
10.	11		
11.	12		
12.	13		

	NUMBER	FACTORS	PRIME OR COMPOSITE?
13.	14		
14.	15		
15.	16		
16.	17		
17.	18		
18.	19		
19.	20		
20.	21		
21.	22		
22.	23		
23.	24		
24.	25		

Using factor trees to find prime factors

Factor Trees

Use the factor tree method to find the prime factors of the following composite numbers.

EXAMPLE: **24**

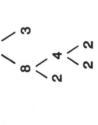

```
      24
     /  \
    8    3
   / \
  2   4
     / \
    2   2
```

Number of Prime Factors (4)

$24 = \underline{(2 \times 2) \times (2 \times 3)}$

$\underline{4 \times 6 = 24}$

Prime Factors

Proof

---

1. **12**

2. **16**

12 = _____ Prime Factors (3)
_____ Proof

16 = _____ Prime Factors (4)
_____ Proof

3. **30**

4. **36**

5. **45**

30 = _____ Prime Factors (3)
_____ Proof

36 = _____ Prime Factors (4)
_____ Proof

45 = _____ Prime Factors (3)
_____ Proof

6. **50**

7. **72**

8. **75**

50 = _____ Prime Factors (3)
_____ Proof

72 = _____ Prime Factors (5)
_____ Proof

75 = _____ Prime Factors (3)
_____ Proof

Using factor trees to find prime factors

NAME _____

Factor Trees

Use the factor tree method to find the prime factors of the following composite numbers.

EXAMPLE: **81**

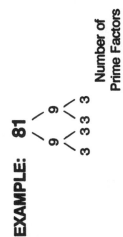

$81 = \underline{3 \times 3 \times 3 \times 3}$ Number of Prime Factors (4)
$\underline{9 \times 9 = 81}$

1. **56**

2. **70**

$56 =$ _____   Prime Factors (4)
       _____   Proof

$70 =$ _____   Prime Factors (3)
       _____   Proof

3. **48**

4. **90**

5. **100**

$48 =$ _____   Prime Factors (5)
       _____   Proof

$90 =$ _____   Prime Factors (4)
       _____   Proof

$100 =$ _____   Prime Factors (4)
        _____   Proof

6. **64**

7. **28**

8. **63**

$64 =$ _____   Prime Factors (6)
       _____   Proof

$28 =$ _____   Prime Factors (3)
       _____   Proof

$63 =$ _____   Prime Factors (3)
       _____   Proof

NAME_____

PRIME FACTORIZATION

Directions: Find the prime factors of the following composite numbers by using factor trees. Work your problems on another sheet of paper and then transfer your answers on to this sheet. *Example is:*

```
      30
      /\
    15  2
    /\
   5  3
```

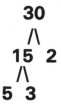

{The prime factors of 30 are 2, 3, and 5 and (2 × 3) × 5 = 30}

1.	42	
2.	33	
3.	36	
4.	72	
5.	48	
6.	50	
7.	45	
8.	64	
9.	81	
10.	20	
11.	100	

Bonus Activity: Using factor trees, find the prime factors of 150, 200, and 1000.

Using the slide method for finding the *GCF, LCM* and fraction in lowest terms   NAME_____

USING THE SLIDE

DIRECTIONS: Examine the method shown below for finding the *greatest common factor, least common multiple, and the fraction in lowest terms* of 36 and 48.

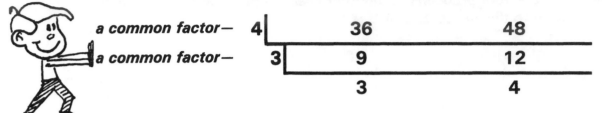

a common factor— 4 | 36   48

a common factor— 3 | 9   12

              3   4

(A) To find the *GCF,* multiply the number outside the steps on the slide on the left side of the table: (4 x 3 = 12).   **(B)** To find the *LCM* , multiply all of the numbers outside of the step of the slide's border: (4 x 3 x 3 x 4 = 144).   **(C)** The fraction, $\frac{36}{48}$, will be shown in lowest terms by the two numbers underneath the slide. Therefore, the fraction is $\frac{3}{4}$ in lowest terms.

		GCF	LCM	Lowest terms			GCF	LCM	Lowest terms
1.	5, 15				10.	14, 35			
2.	3, 24				11.	15, 35			
3.	15, 33				12.	22, 33			
4.	8, 20				13.	15, 25			
5.	18, 45				14	12, 15			
6.	16, 40				15.	16, 20			
7.	15, 37				16.	37, 76			
8.	28, 42				17	49, 63			
9.	14, 49				18.	78, 100			

Using primes, composites, multiples, and factors

NAME _____

ANTICS

DIRECTIONS: To find the entry word for each of the following definitions, solve each problem. Each time your answer occurs in the decoder, write the letter of the problem above it.

What aardvarks like on their pizza :

$\overline{3}$ $\overline{6}$ $\overline{99}$ $\overline{23}$ $\overline{58}$ $\overline{29}$ $\overline{8}$ $\overline{12}$ $\overline{18}$ $\overline{2}$

What aardvarks take for an upset stomach :

$\overline{3}$ $\overline{6}$ $\overline{99}$ $\overline{3}$ $\overline{23}$ $\overline{12}$ $\overline{35}$ $\overline{2}$

Where aardvarks go to ski :

$\overline{3}$ $\overline{6}$ $\overline{99}$ $\overline{3}$ $\overline{11}$ $\overline{23}$ $\overline{99}$ $\overline{12}$ $\overline{23}$ $\overline{3}$

1. Name the greatest common factor of 24 and 36. = _____ I

2. Name a two digit number that is divisible by both 6 and 9. = _____ E

3. Name the largest two digit multiple of 11. = _____ T

4. Name the smallest even number divisible both by 2 and 3. = _____ N

5. Name the prime number between 25 and 30. = _____ O

6. Name the largest composite number between 1 and 60. = _____ H

7. Name the only even prime. = _____ S

8. Name a factor of 24 and 32 that is also a multiple of 8. = _____ V

9. Name a two digit number that is a factor of 22. = _____ R

10. Name a two digit prime number whose digits add up to 5. = _____ C

11. Name a two digit multiple of 7 that its digits add up to 8. = _____ D

12. Name a prime number that is a factor of 12 and 27. = _____ A

Kinesthetic activity involving equivalent fractions

NAME_____

Chocolate Delight

BACKGROUND INFORMATION: This activity will help enhance your students' understanding of equivalent fractions.

DIRECTIONS:

(1) Divide students into groups of 3 or 4. Distribute to each student an 8-1/2" x 11" sheet of paper which then is folded in half. Give each group one Hershey's Milk Chocolate bar. (The one divided into twelve small squares. Mr. Goodbar works, also.)

(2) Ask each student to draw on the front of the paper the wrapper for the Hershey's bar before it is unwrapped.

(3) On the inside cover, students draw the candy bar after it is unwrapped (see below).

(4) On the third part of the paper, they write these fractions and fill in the missing numbers using the candy bar to justify their answers. (They work together to solve the problems.)

$$\frac{1}{4} = \frac{}{12} \qquad \frac{2}{4} = \frac{}{12} \qquad \frac{3}{4} = \frac{}{12} \qquad \frac{1}{6} = \frac{}{12}$$

$$\frac{2}{6} = \frac{}{12} \qquad \frac{5}{6} = \frac{}{12} \qquad \frac{1}{3} = \frac{}{12} \qquad \frac{2}{3} = \frac{}{12}$$

$$\frac{3}{6} = \frac{}{12} \qquad \frac{4}{6} = \frac{}{12} \qquad \frac{6}{6} = \frac{}{12} \qquad \frac{1}{2} = \frac{}{12}$$

(5) On the back of the paper, students write a paragraph explaining how and why they chose the numerators they did to complete the activity.

(6) Once all of these activities are completed, students explain their findings to the teacher, and if he/she is convinced that the group has worked together and everyone in the group has an understanding of the activity, the group can decide how to equally divide the candy bar, and each person can have his/her own "chocolate delight."

NAME_____

Why didn't the skeleton cross the road?

DIRECTIONS: First, solve each problem below. Second, find your answer in the secret code. Third, each time your answer appears in the secret code, write the letter of the problem above it.

1. $\frac{1}{2} = \frac{}{10}$ (T)

2. $\frac{1}{3} = \frac{}{21}$ (Y)

3. $\frac{3}{5} = \frac{}{10}$ (C)

4. $\frac{3}{4} = \frac{}{12}$ (D)

5. $\frac{1}{5} = \frac{}{60}$ (A)

6. $\frac{1}{4} = \frac{}{44}$ (G)

7. $\frac{2}{3} = \frac{}{12}$ (U)

8. $\frac{9}{10} = \frac{}{20}$ (E)

9. $\frac{5}{6} = \frac{}{18}$ (V)

10. $\frac{4}{5} = \frac{}{35}$ (S)

11. $\frac{1}{6} = \frac{}{12}$ (N)

12. $\frac{2}{5} = \frac{}{40}$ (H)

13. $\frac{1}{9} = \frac{}{27}$ (B)

14. $\frac{5}{12} = \frac{}{24}$ (I)

$\overline{\quad}\ \overline{\quad}\ \overline{\quad}\ \overline{\quad}\ \overline{\quad}\ \overline{\quad}\ \overline{\quad}$
3   18   6   12   8   28   18

$\overline{\quad}\ \overline{\quad}\quad\overline{\quad}\ \overline{\quad}\ \overline{\quad}\ \overline{\quad}\ \overline{\quad}$
10   5   9   10   9   2   5

$\overline{\quad}\ \overline{\quad}\ \overline{\quad}\ \overline{\quad}\quad\overline{\quad}\ \overline{\quad}\ \overline{\quad}$
16   12   15   18   12   2   7

$\overline{\quad}\ \overline{\quad}\ \overline{\quad}\ \overline{\quad}$
11   8   5   28

NAME_____

What does a worm do in a corn field?

DIRECTIONS: First, solve each problem below. Second, find your answer in the secret code. Third, each time your answer appears in the secret code, write the letter of the problem above it.

1. $\dfrac{5}{8} = \dfrac{}{24}$ (S)

2. $\dfrac{4}{3} = \dfrac{8}{}$ (T)

3. $\dfrac{3}{5} = \dfrac{12}{}$ (R)

4. $\dfrac{1}{8} = \dfrac{}{32}$ (D)

5. $\dfrac{7}{8} = \dfrac{14}{}$ (H)

6. $\dfrac{2}{3} = \dfrac{8}{}$ (E)

7. $\dfrac{1}{4} = \dfrac{}{12}$ (N)

8. $\dfrac{2}{5} = \dfrac{}{20}$ (G)

9. $\dfrac{0}{4} = \dfrac{}{8}$ (A)

10. $\dfrac{1}{1} = \dfrac{}{7}$ (O)

11. $\dfrac{1}{3} = \dfrac{3}{}$ (U)

12. $\dfrac{3}{8} = \dfrac{9}{}$ (I)

___ ___   ___ ___ ___ ___
16 12   8   7 12 15

___ ___   ___ ___ ___
24   3   7   3 12

___ ___ ___   ___ ___ ___
12   0 20   0   3   4

___ ___ ___   ___ ___ ___
7   9   6   6 16 12

___ ___ ___ ___ ___
7   6 16 12 20

Reducing fractions to lowest terms

NAME _____

Why did Humpty Dumpty have a great fall?

DIRECTIONS: First, reduce each fraction to its lowest terms. Second, find your answer in the secret code. Third, each time your answer appears in the secret code, write the letter of the problem above it.

1. $\dfrac{14}{16}=$ (M)

2. $\dfrac{15}{30}=$ (P)

3. $\dfrac{18}{40}=$ (S)

4. $\dfrac{12}{18}=$ (R)

5. $\dfrac{9}{27}=$ (H)

6. $\dfrac{15}{25}=$ (U)

7. $\dfrac{4}{16}=$ (I)

8. $\dfrac{11}{66}=$ (F)

9. $\dfrac{4}{36}=$ (B)

10. $\dfrac{15}{20}=$ (E)

11. $\dfrac{4}{14}=$ (K)

12. $\dfrac{12}{32}=$ (O)

13. $\dfrac{21}{30}=$ (A)

14. $\dfrac{20}{36}=$ (L)

15. $\dfrac{33}{36}=$ (T)

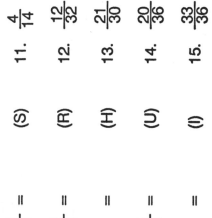

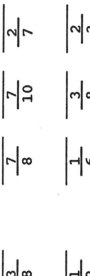

Secret code:

$$\frac{11}{12}\quad \frac{3}{8}\quad \frac{7}{8}\quad \frac{3}{8}\quad \frac{7}{10}\quad \frac{2}{7}\quad \frac{3}{4}$$

$$\frac{3}{5}\quad \frac{1}{2}\quad \frac{1}{6}\quad \frac{1}{3}\quad \frac{2}{3}\quad \frac{1}{4}\quad \frac{1}{3}\quad \frac{5}{9}$$

$$\frac{7}{8}\quad \frac{1}{4}\quad \frac{7}{8}\quad \frac{3}{4}\quad \frac{2}{3}\quad \frac{1}{9}\quad \frac{3}{4}$$

$$\frac{9}{20}\quad \frac{9}{20}\quad \frac{3}{5}\quad \frac{7}{8}\quad \frac{7}{10}\quad \frac{1}{9}\quad \frac{1}{4}$$

$$\frac{7}{8}\quad \frac{2}{3}\quad \frac{9}{20}$$

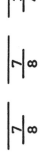

Reducing fractions to lowest terms

What did Mrs. Claus say to her husband during the rainstorm?

DIRECTIONS: First, change each fraction to a mixed number and give the fraction part in its lowest terms. Second, find your answer in the secret code. Third, each time your answer appears in the secret code, write the letter of the problem above it.

1. $\dfrac{9}{8}$ = (M)

2. $\dfrac{39}{4}$ = (D)

3. $\dfrac{61}{2}$ = (K)

4. $\dfrac{9}{4}$ = (T)

5. $\dfrac{20}{8}$ = (O)

6. $\dfrac{24}{9}$ = (A)

7. $\dfrac{26}{8}$ = (E)

8. $\dfrac{7}{3}$ = (N)

9. $\dfrac{42}{20}$ = (I)

10. $\dfrac{17}{9}$ = (C)

11. $\dfrac{12}{7}$ = (R)

12. $\dfrac{36}{8}$ = (L)

13. $\dfrac{35}{10}$ = (H)

Secret code:

$\overline{\ }\ \overline{\ }\ \overline{\ }\ \overline{\ }\ \overline{\ }$
$1\tfrac{8}{9}\quad 2\tfrac{1}{2}\quad 2\tfrac{1}{2}\quad 1\tfrac{1}{8}\quad 2\tfrac{2}{3}\quad 2\tfrac{1}{3}\quad 9\tfrac{3}{4}$

$\overline{\ }\ \overline{\ }\ \overline{\ }\ \overline{\ }\ \overline{\ }$
$3\tfrac{1}{4}\quad 2\tfrac{1}{2}\quad 2\tfrac{1}{2}\quad 30\tfrac{1}{2}\quad 3\tfrac{1}{4}$

$\overline{\ }\ \overline{\ }\ \overline{\ }\ \overline{\ }$
$2\tfrac{2}{3}\quad 2\tfrac{1}{4}\quad 3\tfrac{1}{2}\quad 2\tfrac{1}{4}$

$\overline{\ }\ \overline{\ }\ \overline{\ }\ \overline{\ }\ \overline{\ }$
$2\tfrac{1}{10}\quad 2\tfrac{1}{3}\quad 9\tfrac{3}{4}\quad 3\tfrac{1}{4}\quad 3\tfrac{1}{4}$

$\overline{\ }\ \overline{\ }\ \overline{\ }\ \overline{\ }$
$1\tfrac{5}{7}\quad 3\tfrac{1}{4}\quad 1\tfrac{5}{7}$

Why did the umpire throw the chicken out of the game?

DIRECTIONS: First, reduce each fraction to its lowest terms. Second, find your answer in the secret code. Third, each time your answer appears in the secret code, write the letter of the problem above it.

1. $\dfrac{6}{10}$ = _____ (D)

2. $\dfrac{8}{16}$ = _____ (S)

3. $\dfrac{9}{27}$ = _____ (Y)

4. $\dfrac{12}{16}$ = _____ (L)

5. $\dfrac{2}{18}$ = _____ (F)

6. $\dfrac{15}{18}$ = _____ (T)

7. $\dfrac{28}{48}$ = _____ (C)

8. $\dfrac{10}{15}$ = _____ (P)

9. $\dfrac{6}{24}$ = _____ (H)

10. $\dfrac{14}{48}$ = _____ (O)

11. $\dfrac{9}{30}$ = _____ (U)

12. $\dfrac{22}{24}$ = _____ (A)

13. $\dfrac{27}{48}$ = _____ (E)

14. $\dfrac{50}{70}$ = _____ (W)

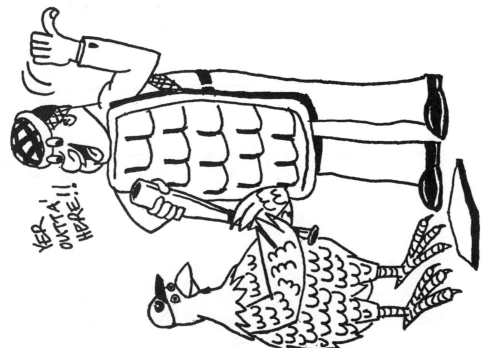

Secret code:

$\dfrac{1}{9}$	$\dfrac{7}{24}$	$\dfrac{5}{7}$	$\dfrac{3}{4}$	$\dfrac{3}{10}$	$\dfrac{7}{24}$	$\dfrac{2}{3}$	$\dfrac{11}{12}$	$\dfrac{1}{3}$	$\dfrac{3}{5}$
$\dfrac{1}{4}$	$\dfrac{9}{16}$		$\dfrac{1}{2}$		$\dfrac{9}{16}$	$\dfrac{2}{3}$	$\dfrac{9}{16}$	$\dfrac{7}{12}$	$\dfrac{9}{16}$
			$\dfrac{1}{2}$		$\dfrac{1}{2}$	$\dfrac{3}{4}$	$\dfrac{2}{3}$		$\dfrac{5}{6}$

NAME_____

Ghoulish Definitions

DIRECTIONS: To find the meaning of each of the ghoulish definitions listed below, first change each fraction to a mixed numeral and your answer should be in lowest terms. Second, find your answer in the secret code. Third, each time your answer appears in the secret code, write the letter of the problem above it.

1. $\frac{7}{3}$ = _____ O

2. $\frac{12}{4}$ = _____ L

3. $\frac{8}{6}$ = _____ B

4. $\frac{15}{12}$ = _____ D

5. $\frac{22}{10}$ = _____ N

6. $\frac{13}{11}$ = _____ G

7. $\frac{15}{10}$ = _____ U

8. $\frac{39}{15}$ = _____ H

9. $\frac{40}{15}$ = _____ A

A VAMPIRE'S DOG: $\overline{\hphantom{xx}}$
                       $2\frac{2}{3}$

$\overline{\hphantom{xx}}$ $\overline{\hphantom{xx}}$ $\overline{\hphantom{xx}}$ $\overline{\hphantom{xx}}$ $\overline{\hphantom{xx}}$ $\overline{\hphantom{xx}}$ $\overline{\hphantom{xx}}$ $\overline{\hphantom{xx}}$ $\overline{\hphantom{xx}}$ $\overline{\hphantom{xx}}$
$1\frac{1}{3}$ 3 $2\frac{1}{3}$ $2\frac{1}{3}$ $1\frac{1}{4}$ $2\frac{3}{5}$ $2\frac{1}{3}$ $1\frac{1}{2}$ $2\frac{1}{5}$ $1\frac{1}{4}$

A WITCH'S PURSE: $\overline{\hphantom{xx}}$
                       $2\frac{2}{3}$

$\overline{\hphantom{xx}}$ $\overline{\hphantom{xx}}$ $\overline{\hphantom{xx}}$ $\overline{\hphantom{xx}}$ $\overline{\hphantom{xx}}$ $\overline{\hphantom{xx}}$
$2\frac{3}{5}$ $2\frac{2}{3}$ $1\frac{2}{11}$ $1\frac{1}{3}$ $2\frac{2}{3}$ $1\frac{2}{11}$

Cnanging fractions to whole numbers or mixed numerals

NAME_____

DAFFY DEFINITIONS

DIRECTIONS: First, solve each problem below. Second, find your answer in the secret code. Third, each time your answer appears in the secret code, write the letter of the problem above it.

1. $\frac{15}{2}$ = _____ G

2. $\frac{8}{3}$ = _____ T

3. $\frac{21}{5}$ = _____ C

4. $\frac{9}{3}$ = _____ M

5. $\frac{14}{3}$ = _____ L

6. $\frac{10}{2}$ = _____ O

7. $\frac{22}{7}$ = _____ U

8. $\frac{36}{8}$ = _____ R

9. $\frac{13}{9}$ = _____ S

10. $\frac{22}{6}$ = _____ K

11. $\frac{72}{8}$ = _____ I

12. $\frac{100}{50}$ = _____ H

13. $\frac{43}{7}$ = _____ A

14. $\frac{34}{5}$ = _____ F

15. $\frac{33}{10}$ = _____ E

16. $\frac{22}{16}$ = _____ N

17. $\frac{42}{15}$ = _____ X

18. $\frac{31}{10}$ = _____ Y

METRIC COOKIE:

$\overline{\quad}$ $\overline{\quad}$ $\overline{\quad}$ $\overline{\quad}$ $\overline{\quad}$
$6\frac{1}{7}$ $\quad$ $7\frac{1}{2}$ $4\frac{1}{2}$ $6\frac{1}{7}$ 3

$\overline{\quad}$ $\overline{\quad}$ $\overline{\quad}$ $\overline{\quad}$ $\overline{\quad}$ $\overline{\quad}$ $\overline{\quad}$
$4\frac{1}{5}$ $4\frac{1}{2}$ $6\frac{1}{7}$ $4\frac{1}{5}$ $3\frac{2}{3}$ $3\frac{3}{10}$ $4\frac{1}{2}$

DECLARATION OF INDEPENDENCE:

$\overline{\quad}$ $\overline{\quad}$ $\overline{\quad}$ $\overline{\quad}$ $\overline{\quad}$
$6\frac{1}{7}$ $\quad$ $1\frac{3}{8}$ 5 $2\frac{2}{3}$ $3\frac{3}{10}$

$\overline{\quad}$ $\overline{\quad}$ $\overline{\quad}$ $\overline{\quad}$ $\overline{\quad}$ $\overline{\quad}$ $\overline{\quad}$ $\overline{\quad}$
$3\frac{3}{10}$ $2\frac{4}{5}$ $4\frac{1}{5}$ $3\frac{1}{7}$ $1\frac{4}{9}$ 9 $1\frac{3}{8}$ $7\frac{1}{2}$

$\overline{\quad}$ $\overline{\quad}$ $\overline{\quad}$ $\overline{\quad}$ $\overline{\quad}$ $\overline{\quad}$ $\overline{\quad}$
$3\frac{1}{10}$ 5 $3\frac{1}{7}$ $6\frac{4}{5}$ $4\frac{1}{2}$ 5 3

$\overline{\quad}$ $\overline{\quad}$ $\overline{\quad}$ $\overline{\quad}$ $\overline{\quad}$ $\overline{\quad}$
$1\frac{4}{9}$ $4\frac{1}{5}$ 2 5 5 $4\frac{2}{3}$

NAME_____

Phobias!
Phobias!
Phobias!

Phobia: Fear of

DIRECTIONS: To find the meaning of each of the phobias listed below, first change each mixed numeral to a fraction. Second, find your answer in the secret code. Third, each time your answer appears in the secret code, write the letter of the problem above it.

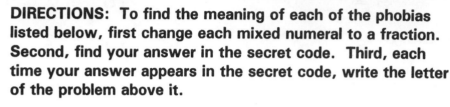

6. $2\frac{1}{2}$ = _____ M

1. $3\frac{2}{3}$ = _____ R

7. $3\frac{3}{10}$ = _____ I

2. $6\frac{1}{4}$ = _____ H

8. $3\frac{1}{3}$ = _____ E

3. $2\frac{1}{3}$ = _____ B

9. $4\frac{2}{5}$ = _____ U

4. $6\frac{1}{7}$ = _____ N

10. $8\frac{1}{2}$ = _____ T

5. $1\frac{1}{4}$ = _____ G

11. $10\frac{1}{3}$ = _____ O

12. $6\frac{2}{7}$ = _____ F   13. $8\frac{3}{7}$ = _____ S   14. $1\frac{1}{9}$ = _____ A

ACROPHOBIA: $\dfrac{44}{7}$ $\dfrac{10}{3}$ $\dfrac{10}{9}$ $\dfrac{11}{3}$ $\dfrac{31}{3}$ $\dfrac{44}{7}$

$\dfrac{25}{4}$ $\dfrac{10}{3}$ $\dfrac{33}{10}$ $\dfrac{5}{4}$ $\dfrac{25}{4}$ $\dfrac{17}{2}$ $\dfrac{59}{7}$

TRISKAIDEKAPHOBIA: $\dfrac{44}{7}$ $\dfrac{10}{3}$ $\dfrac{10}{9}$ $\dfrac{11}{3}$ $\dfrac{31}{3}$ $\dfrac{44}{7}$

$\dfrac{17}{2}$ $\dfrac{25}{4}$ $\dfrac{10}{3}$ $\dfrac{43}{7}$ $\dfrac{22}{5}$ $\dfrac{5}{2}$ $\dfrac{7}{3}$ $\dfrac{10}{3}$ $\dfrac{11}{3}$

$\dfrac{17}{2}$ $\dfrac{25}{4}$ $\dfrac{33}{10}$ $\dfrac{11}{3}$ $\dfrac{17}{2}$ $\dfrac{10}{3}$ $\dfrac{10}{3}$ $\dfrac{43}{7}$

How many months have 28 days?

DIRECTIONS: By finding a common denominator for a pair of fractions, you can determine which one is the greatest. Study this example:

Which is the greatest $\frac{2}{3}$ or $\frac{3}{4}$?

$$\frac{2}{3} = \frac{8}{12}$$

$$\frac{3}{4} = \frac{9}{12}$$

Therefore, $\frac{3}{4}$ is greater than $\frac{2}{3}$ by $\frac{1}{12}$.

Find the greater fraction in each of the pairs below. Each time your answer occurs in the decoder, write the letter of the problem above it.

1. $\frac{2}{3}$ or $\frac{5}{8}$ = _____ E

2. $\frac{5}{6}$ or $\frac{7}{8}$ = _____ F

3. $\frac{2}{5}$ or $\frac{3}{6}$ = _____ S

4. $\frac{7}{9}$ or $\frac{6}{8}$ = _____ L

5. $\frac{4}{5}$ or $\frac{2}{3}$ = _____ N

6. $\frac{5}{7}$ or $\frac{5}{6}$ = _____ T

7. $\frac{2}{4}$ or $\frac{4}{9}$ = _____ H

8. $\frac{1}{3}$ or $\frac{2}{9}$ = _____ D

9. $\frac{4}{6}$ or $\frac{5}{9}$ = _____ M

10. $\frac{5}{8}$ or $\frac{5}{7}$ = _____ A

11. $\frac{3}{8}$ or $\frac{4}{9}$ = _____ O

$\frac{5}{7}$ $\frac{7}{9}$ $\frac{7}{9}$ $\frac{4}{9}$ $\frac{7}{8}$ $\frac{5}{6}$ $\frac{2}{4}$ $\frac{2}{3}$

$\frac{4}{6}$ $\frac{4}{9}$ $\frac{4}{5}$ $\frac{5}{6}$ $\frac{2}{4}$ $\frac{3}{6}$ $\frac{1}{3}$ $\frac{4}{9}$

Adding like fractions with no regrouping

What happens when the frog's car breaks down?

DIRECTIONS: First, solve each problem below. Second, find your answer in the secret code. Third, each time your answer appears in the secret code, write the letter of the problem above it.

1. $\dfrac{6}{11}$
    $+\ \dfrac{2}{11}$
    _____ = D

2. $\dfrac{1}{3}$
    $+\ \dfrac{1}{3}$
    _____ = Y

3. $\dfrac{7}{12}$
    $+\ \dfrac{4}{12}$
    _____ = T

4. $\dfrac{4}{9}$
    $+\ \dfrac{3}{9}$
    _____ = W

5. $\dfrac{1}{4}$
    $+\ \dfrac{2}{4}$
    _____ = G

6. $\dfrac{5}{6}$
    $+\ \dfrac{0}{6}$
    _____ = O

7. $\dfrac{7}{10}$
    $+\ \dfrac{2}{10}$
    _____ = S

8. $\dfrac{1}{5}$
    $+\ \dfrac{2}{5}$
    _____ = A

9. $\dfrac{5}{8}$
    $+\ \dfrac{2}{8}$
    _____ = H

10. $\dfrac{7}{15}$
    $+\ \dfrac{6}{15}$
    _____ = E

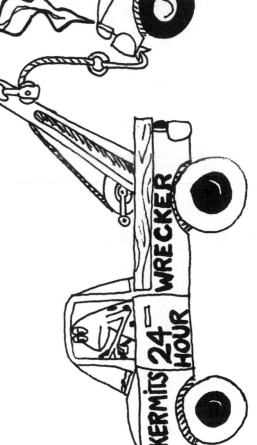

$\dfrac{7}{8}\ \ \dfrac{13}{15}$

$\dfrac{3}{4}\ \ \dfrac{13}{15}\ \ \dfrac{11}{12}\ \ \dfrac{9}{10}$

$\dfrac{11}{12}\ \ \dfrac{5}{6}\ \ \dfrac{3}{5}\ \ \dfrac{8}{11}$

$\dfrac{3}{5}\ \ \dfrac{7}{9}\ \ \dfrac{3}{5}\ \ \dfrac{2}{3}$

Why did the astronaut take a shovel into space?

DIRECTIONS: First, solve each problem below on another sheet of paper. Second, find your answer in the secret code. Third, each time your answer appears in the secret code, write the letter of the problem above it.

1. $\frac{3}{8} + \frac{2}{8} =$ _____ (G)

2. $\frac{7}{9} - \frac{3}{9} =$ _____ (L)

3. $\frac{3}{7} + \frac{1}{7} =$ _____ (C)

4. $\frac{11}{30} + \frac{12}{30} =$ _____ (E)

5. $\frac{27}{38} - \frac{10}{38} =$ _____ (I)

6. $\frac{2}{9} + \frac{5}{9} =$ _____ (A)

7. $\frac{16}{37} + \frac{10}{37} =$ _____ (K)

8. $\frac{26}{15} - \frac{13}{15} =$ _____ (O)

9. $\frac{18}{25} + \frac{19}{25} =$ _____ (D)

10. $\frac{8}{8} - \frac{5}{8} =$ _____ (H)

11. $\frac{19}{20} - \frac{10}{20} =$ _____ (T)

12. $\frac{10}{43} + \frac{21}{43} =$ _____ (B)

$\frac{9}{20}$ $\frac{13}{15}$ $\frac{37}{25}$ $\frac{31}{43}$ $\frac{7}{9}$ $\frac{4}{9}$ $\frac{7}{9}$ $\frac{4}{7}$ $\frac{26}{37}$

$\frac{3}{8}$ $\frac{13}{15}$ $\frac{4}{9}$ $\frac{23}{30}$ $\frac{5}{8}$ $\frac{17}{38}$

Adding and subtracting fractions with like denominators

©1995 by Incentive Publications, Inc., Nashville, TN.

NAME_____

Why is six afraid of seven?

DIRECTIONS: First, solve each problem below. Second, find your answer in the secret code. Third, each time your answer appears in the secret code, write the letter of the problem above it.

1. $\frac{3}{4} + \frac{2}{5}$ = _____(T)

2. $\frac{3}{8} + \frac{2}{3}$ = _____(I)

3. $\frac{1}{2} + \frac{2}{3}$ = _____(U)

4. $\frac{4}{3} + \frac{3}{4}$ = _____(S)

5. $\frac{5}{9} + \frac{2}{3}$ = _____(A)

6. $\frac{3}{8} + \frac{1}{3}$ = _____(V)

7. $\frac{1}{2} + \frac{5}{6}$ = _____(C)

8. $\frac{5}{8} + \frac{2}{3}$ = _____(E)

9. $\frac{2}{3} + \frac{3}{2}$ = _____(B)

10. $\frac{1}{5} + \frac{2}{7}$ = _____(N)

$\overline{}$ $2\frac{1}{6}$ $\overline{}$ $1\frac{7}{24}$ $\overline{}$ $1\frac{1}{3}$ $\overline{}$ $1\frac{2}{9}$ $\overline{}$ $1\frac{1}{6}$ $\overline{}$ $2\frac{1}{12}$ $\overline{}$ $1\frac{7}{24}$

$\overline{}$ $2\frac{1}{12}$ $\overline{}$ $1\frac{7}{24}$ $\overline{}$ $\frac{17}{24}$ $\overline{}$ $1\frac{7}{24}$ $\overline{}$ $\frac{17}{35}$

$\overline{}$ $1\frac{2}{9}$ $\overline{}$ $1\frac{3}{20}$ $\overline{}$ $1\frac{7}{24}$

$\overline{}$ $\frac{17}{35}$ $\overline{}$ $1\frac{1}{24}$ $\overline{}$ $\frac{17}{35}$ $\overline{}$ $1\frac{7}{24}$

Subtracting fractions with unlike denominators

Why did the Cyclops have to close his school?

DIRECTIONS: First, solve each problem below on another sheet of paper. Second, find your answer in the secret code. Third, each time your answer appears in the secret code, write the letter of the problem above it.

1. $\frac{7}{8} - \frac{1}{4} =$ ___ L

2. $\frac{13}{15} - \frac{7}{10} =$ ___ A

3. $\frac{7}{9} - \frac{1}{3} =$ ___ S

4. $\frac{11}{12} - \frac{2}{3} =$ ___ N

5. $\frac{13}{14} - \frac{1}{7} =$ ___ U

6. $\frac{9}{10} - \frac{3}{4} =$ ___ C

7. $\frac{19}{20} - \frac{3}{4} =$ ___ D

8. $\frac{7}{9} - \frac{2}{3} =$ ___ B

9. $\frac{10}{11} - \frac{2}{3} =$ ___ E

10. $\frac{8}{7} - \frac{12}{21} =$ ___ I

11. $\frac{5}{4} - \frac{1}{2} =$ ___ H

12. $\frac{4}{4} - \frac{1}{2} =$ ___ Y

13. $\frac{23}{24} - \frac{11}{12} =$ ___ O

14. $\frac{23}{21} - \frac{3}{7} =$ ___ P

Secret code:

___	___	___	___	___	___
$\frac{1}{9}$	$\frac{8}{33}$	$\frac{3}{20}$	$\frac{1}{6}$	$\frac{11}{14}$	$\frac{8}{33}$

___	___	___	___	___	___	___
$\frac{3}{4}$	$\frac{8}{33}$	$\frac{3}{4}$	$\frac{1}{6}$	$\frac{1}{5}$	$\frac{4}{9}$	$\frac{8}{33}$

___	___	___	___	___	___	___
$\frac{1}{24}$	$\frac{1}{4}$	$\frac{5}{8}$	$\frac{1}{2}$	$\frac{1}{2}$	$\frac{1}{24}$	$\frac{1}{4}$

___	___	___	___	___
$\frac{2}{3}$	$\frac{11}{14}$	$\frac{2}{3}$	$\frac{4}{7}$	$\frac{5}{8}$

©1995 by Incentive Publications, Inc., Nashville, TN.

NAME _____

Subtracting fractions with unlike denominators

What's the only thing to eat
on a deserted island?

DIRECTIONS: First, solve each problem below on another sheet of paper. Second, find your answer in the secret code. Third, each time your answer appears in the secret code, write the letter of the problem above it.

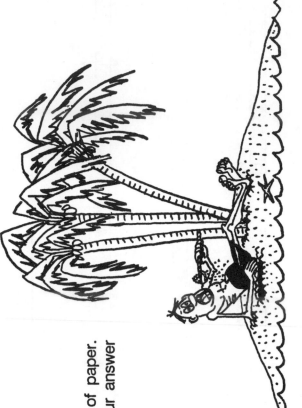

1. $\dfrac{14}{15} - \dfrac{1}{5} = \underline{\quad}$ Y

2. $\dfrac{17}{20} - \dfrac{1}{10} = \underline{\quad}$ H

3. $\dfrac{19}{20} - \dfrac{3}{4} = \underline{\quad}$ N

4. $\dfrac{4}{3} - \dfrac{5}{6} = \underline{\quad}$ R

5. $\dfrac{5}{4} - \dfrac{5}{8} = \underline{\quad}$ S

6. $\dfrac{9}{8} - \dfrac{7}{8} = \underline{\quad}$ A

7. $\dfrac{13}{12} - \dfrac{1}{4} = \underline{\quad}$ W

8. $\dfrac{5}{6} - \dfrac{1}{4} = \underline{\quad}$ I

9. $\dfrac{5}{8} - \dfrac{1}{4} = \underline{\quad}$ T

10. $\dfrac{1}{2} - \dfrac{3}{8} = \underline{\quad}$ C

11. $\dfrac{13}{15} - \dfrac{1}{5} = \underline{\quad}$ O

12. $\dfrac{4}{5} - \dfrac{1}{4} = \underline{\quad}$ E

13. $\dfrac{3}{4} - \dfrac{7}{10} = \underline{\quad}$ L

14. $\dfrac{6}{7} - \dfrac{1}{3} = \underline{\quad}$ D

$\overline{\dfrac{2}{3}}\ \overline{\dfrac{1}{5}}\ \overline{\dfrac{11}{15}}\ \overline{\dfrac{1}{20}}\ \overline{\dfrac{11}{15}}\ \overline{\dfrac{3}{8}}\ \overline{\dfrac{11}{20}}\ \overline{\dfrac{3}{4}}\ \overline{\dfrac{5}{8}}\ \overline{\dfrac{1}{4}}\ \overline{\dfrac{11}{21}}$

$\overline{\dfrac{5}{6}}\ \overline{\dfrac{3}{4}}\ \overline{\dfrac{7}{12}}\ \overline{\dfrac{1}{8}}\ \overline{\dfrac{7}{12}}\ \overline{\dfrac{3}{4}}\ \overline{\dfrac{5}{8}}\ \overline{\dfrac{3}{8}}\ \overline{\dfrac{1}{5}}\ \overline{\dfrac{11}{20}}\ \overline{\dfrac{1}{2}}$

$\overline{\dfrac{3}{4}}\ \overline{\dfrac{11}{20}}$

Adding mixed numerals with no regrouping

What is the nationality of Santa Claus?

DIRECTIONS: First, solve each problem below. Second, find your answer in the secret code. Third, each time your answer appears in the secret code, write the letter of the problem above it.

1. $3\frac{1}{3}$
    $+ 4\frac{1}{3}$
    _____ = **L**

2. $4\frac{1}{3}$
    $+ 2\frac{1}{8}$
    _____ = **P**

3. $8\frac{1}{3}$
    $+ 7\frac{1}{2}$
    _____ = **I**

4. $6\frac{1}{3}$
    $+ 3\frac{1}{4}$
    _____ = **N**

5. $7\frac{1}{9}$
    $+ 4\frac{2}{3}$
    _____ = **R**

6. $3\frac{3}{9}$
    $+ 2\frac{1}{3}$
    _____ = **O**

7. $6\frac{2}{5}$
    $+ 4\frac{1}{2}$
    _____ = **S**

8. $3\frac{4}{9}$
    $+ 1\frac{1}{3}$
    _____ = **T**

9. $2\frac{1}{4}$
    $+ 3\frac{1}{4}$
    _____ = **E**

10. $3\frac{1}{7}$
    $+ 2\frac{2}{3}$
    _____ = **H**

$5\frac{17}{21}$	$5\frac{1}{2}$		$15\frac{5}{6}$	$10\frac{9}{10}$	

$9\frac{7}{12}$	$5\frac{2}{3}$	$11\frac{7}{9}$	$4\frac{7}{9}$	$5\frac{17}{21}$	

$6\frac{11}{24}$	$5\frac{2}{3}$	$7\frac{2}{3}$	$15\frac{5}{6}$	$10\frac{9}{10}$	$5\frac{17}{21}$

Adding mixed numerals with regrouping

NAME _____

Where is the only place in the world an elephant can visit the dentist?

DIRECTIONS: First, solve each problem below on another sheet of paper. Second, find your answer in the secret code. Third, each time your answer appears in the secret code, write the letter of the problem above it.

9. $3\frac{5}{7} + 2\frac{3}{8} =$ _____ (T)

1. $1\frac{3}{4} + 2\frac{1}{3} =$ _____ (S)

2. $2\frac{1}{5} + 3\frac{5}{6} =$ _____ (L)

3. $7\frac{1}{8} + 2\frac{3}{4} + 1\frac{1}{3} =$ _____ (C)

4. $5\frac{3}{7} + 3\frac{2}{3} =$ _____ (M)

5. $10\frac{5}{12} + 2\frac{3}{5} + 4\frac{1}{6} =$ _____ (B)

6. $8\frac{1}{2} + \frac{1}{3} + 6\frac{11}{12} =$ _____ (U)

7. $13\frac{1}{9} + 2\frac{2}{3} + 1\frac{1}{2} =$ _____ (O)

8. $8\frac{3}{8} + 1\frac{1}{4} + 3\frac{5}{12} =$ _____ (A)

$6\frac{5}{56}$ $15\frac{3}{4}$ $4\frac{1}{12}$ $11\frac{5}{24}$ $13\frac{1}{24}$ $6\frac{1}{30}$ $17\frac{5}{18}$ $13\frac{1}{24}$ $4\frac{1}{12}$ $13\frac{1}{24}$

$13\frac{1}{24}$ $6\frac{1}{30}$ $13\frac{1}{24}$ $17\frac{11}{60}$ $13\frac{1}{24}$ $9\frac{2}{21}$ $17\frac{5}{18}$ $13\frac{1}{24}$

Where is the coldest place in the theater?

32

DIRECTIONS: First, solve each problem below. Second, find your answer in the secret code. Third, each time your answer appears in the secret code, write the letter of the problem above it.

1.
$$1\frac{1}{4}$$
$$2\frac{1}{2}$$
$$+\ 5\frac{3}{5}$$
= R

2.
$$4\frac{2}{3}$$
$$4\frac{1}{6}$$
$$5\frac{1}{2}$$
$$+\ 3\frac{7}{12}$$
= W

3.
$$2\frac{3}{5}$$
$$8\frac{5}{6}$$
$$2\frac{7}{15}$$
$$+\ 3\frac{1}{3}$$
= N

4.
$$5\frac{1}{4}$$
$$2\frac{5}{12}$$
$$9\frac{1}{10}$$
$$+\ 2\frac{3}{5}$$
= O

5.
$$4\frac{1}{3}$$
$$\frac{3}{8}$$
$$6\frac{5}{12}$$
$$+\ 1\frac{5}{24}$$
= I

6.
$$7\frac{1}{9}$$
$$2\frac{5}{12}$$
$$6\frac{1}{3}$$
$$+\ 2\frac{3}{4}$$
= Z

$$12\ \frac{1}{3} \qquad 17\ \frac{7}{30} \qquad 18\ \frac{11}{18} \qquad 9\ \frac{7}{20} \qquad 19\ \frac{11}{30} \qquad 17\ \frac{11}{12}$$

Subtracting mixed numerals with regrouping

NAME _____

What's grey, heavy and sends people to sleep?

DIRECTIONS: First, solve each problem below. Second, find your answer in the secret code. Third, each time your answer appears in the secret code, write the letter of the problem above it.

1. $6\frac{1}{2}$
    $-\ 3\frac{3}{4}$
    $= P$

2. $7\frac{5}{9}$
    $-\ 6\frac{2}{3}$
    $= S$

3. $8\frac{1}{4}$
    $-\ 5\frac{5}{6}$
    $= A$

4. 6
    $-\ 3\frac{2}{3}$
    $= T$

5. 12
    $-\ 4\frac{4}{5}$
    $= U$

6. $10\frac{1}{7}$
    $-\ 2\frac{2}{3}$
    $= N$

7. $54\frac{1}{8}$
    $-\ 42\frac{1}{3}$
    $= M$

8. $16\frac{2}{13}$
    $-\ 14\frac{7}{26}$
    $= M$

9. $12\frac{5}{8}$
    $-\ 9\frac{2}{3}$
    $= Y$

10. $24\frac{1}{12}$
    $-\ 19\frac{3}{5}$
    $= O$

$= H$

$2\frac{5}{12}$ | $4\frac{29}{60}$ | $1\frac{23}{26}$ | $2\frac{3}{4}$ | $7\frac{10}{21}$ | $2\frac{23}{24}$ | $2\frac{3}{4}$ | $2\frac{23}{24}$ | $2\frac{5}{12}$ | $2\frac{1}{3}$ | $11\frac{19}{24}$ | $7\frac{1}{5}$ | $\frac{8}{9}$

NAME_____

How do Martian cowboys greet each other?

DIRECTIONS: First, solve each problem below. Second, find your answer in the secret code. Third, each time your answer appears in the secret code, write the letter of the problem above it.

1. $6\frac{1}{3} - 2\frac{2}{3}$ = _____ G

2. $3\frac{2}{4} - 1\frac{1}{2}$ = _____ H

3. $5\frac{2}{5} - \frac{2}{3}$ = _____ S

4. $8\frac{3}{10} - 2\frac{5}{10}$ = _____ N

5. $9\frac{1}{2} - 3\frac{2}{3}$ = _____ L

6. $12\frac{1}{4} - 2\frac{3}{4}$ = _____ T

7. $4\frac{3}{5} - 1\frac{3}{4}$ = _____ O

8. $20\frac{1}{8} - 3\frac{3}{4}$ = _____ I

9. $16\frac{1}{10} - \frac{7}{15}$ = _____ W

10. $9\frac{1}{6} - 7\frac{5}{6}$ = _____ C

11. $8\frac{1}{7} - 3\frac{5}{7}$ = _____ M

12. $8\frac{1}{4} - 5\frac{3}{7}$ = _____ D

13. $9 - 1\frac{3}{4}$ = _____ E

14. $3\frac{3}{5} - 2\frac{6}{10}$ = _____ U

15. $7\frac{1}{3} - 4\frac{2}{3}$ = _____ A

$\overline{}$ $\overline{}$ $\overline{}$ $\overline{}$
$15\frac{19}{30}$ $16\frac{3}{8}$ $9\frac{1}{2}$ 2

$\overline{}$ $\overline{}$ $\overline{}$ $\overline{}$ $\overline{}$ $\overline{}$ $\overline{}$ $\overline{}$ $\overline{}$ $\overline{}$ $\overline{}$ $\overline{}$ $\overline{}$
$1\frac{1}{3}$ $2\frac{17}{20}$ $4\frac{3}{7}$ $4\frac{3}{7}$ 1 $5\frac{4}{5}$ $16\frac{3}{8}$ $1\frac{1}{3}$ $2\frac{2}{3}$ $9\frac{1}{2}$ $16\frac{3}{8}$ $2\frac{17}{20}$ $5\frac{4}{5}$

$\overline{}$ $\overline{}$ $\overline{}$ $\overline{}$ $\overline{}$ $\overline{}$ $\overline{}$ $\overline{}$ $\overline{}$ $\overline{}$ $\overline{}$
$4\frac{11}{15}$ $2\frac{2}{3}$ $2\frac{23}{28}$ $2\frac{23}{28}$ $5\frac{5}{6}$ $7\frac{1}{4}$ $5\frac{5}{6}$ $16\frac{3}{8}$ $3\frac{2}{3}$ 2 $9\frac{1}{2}$ $4\frac{11}{15}$

NAME_____

What meal did the Revolutionists serve to catch spies?

DIRECTIONS: First, solve each problem below. Second, find your answer in the secret code. Third, each time your answer appears in the secret code, write the letter of the problem above it.

1. $6\frac{1}{5} + 2\frac{2}{3}$ = _____ R

2. $4\frac{5}{8} + 1\frac{3}{4}$ = _____ K

3. $4\frac{1}{4} - 2\frac{11}{20}$ = _____ Y

4. $8\frac{1}{6} + 7\frac{2}{3} + 4\frac{1}{2}$ = _____ I

5. $9\frac{1}{6} - 7\frac{5}{6}$ = _____ O

6. $2\frac{13}{20} + 5\frac{3}{5}$ = _____ A

7. $2\frac{5}{6} + 3\frac{2}{5}$ = _____ N

8. $8\frac{11}{14} - 3\frac{6}{7}$ = _____ H

9. $3\frac{1}{3} + 2\frac{1}{2} + 5\frac{5}{6}$ = _____ E

10. $9\frac{2}{7} - 1\frac{1}{3}$ = _____ C

11. $12\frac{3}{8} - 4\frac{3}{4}$ = _____ T

$\overline{\quad\quad} \ 7\frac{20}{21}$ $\overline{\quad\quad} \ 4\frac{13}{14}$ $\overline{\quad\quad} \ 20\frac{1}{3}$ $\overline{\quad\quad} \ 7\frac{20}{21}$ $\overline{\quad\quad} \ 6\frac{3}{8}$ $\overline{\quad\quad} \ 11\frac{2}{3}$ $\overline{\quad\quad} \ 6\frac{7}{30}$

$\overline{\quad\quad} \ 7\frac{20}{21}$ $\overline{\quad\quad} \ 8\frac{1}{4}$ $\overline{\quad\quad} \ 7\frac{5}{8}$ $\overline{\quad\quad} \ 7\frac{20}{21}$ $\overline{\quad\quad} \ 4\frac{13}{14}$ $\overline{\quad\quad} \ 8\frac{1}{4}$

$\overline{\quad\quad} \ 7\frac{5}{8}$ $\overline{\quad\quad} \ 1\frac{1}{3}$ $\overline{\quad\quad} \ 8\frac{13}{15}$ $\overline{\quad\quad} \ 1\frac{7}{10}$

Adding and subtracting fractions with regrouping

NAME_____

What did one magnet say to the other magnet?

DIRECTIONS: Solve each problem, and each time your answer appears in the decoder, write the letter of the problem above it.

1. $8\frac{1}{4} - 4\frac{5}{6} =$ _____ F

2. $9\frac{5}{12} + 2\frac{3}{5} + 1\frac{1}{6} =$ _____ O

3. $\frac{3}{4} + \frac{7}{10} =$ _____ R

4. $6\frac{1}{3} + 3\frac{1}{4} =$ _____ I

5. $\frac{13}{15} - \frac{1}{5} =$ _____ Y

6. $1\frac{1}{5} + 3\frac{5}{6} =$ _____ V

7. $12\frac{5}{8} - 8\frac{2}{3} =$ _____ C

8. $8 - 4\frac{4}{5} =$ _____ E

9. $\frac{3}{4} + \frac{1}{5} + \frac{7}{10} =$ _____ N

10. $7 + 8\frac{2}{3} =$ _____ U

11. $16\frac{1}{13} - 14\frac{7}{26} =$ _____ D

12. $5\frac{1}{4} + 2\frac{5}{12} + 3\frac{1}{10} + 1\frac{3}{5} =$ _____ A

13. $12 - \frac{2}{3} =$ _____ T

$\overline{\quad 9\frac{7}{12} \quad}$ $\overline{\quad 3\frac{5}{12} \quad}$ $\overline{\quad 9\frac{7}{12} \quad}$ $\overline{\quad 1\frac{13}{20} \quad}$ $\overline{\quad 1\frac{21}{26} \quad}$

$\overline{\quad \frac{2}{3} \quad}$ $\overline{\quad 13\frac{11}{60} \quad}$ $\overline{\quad 15\frac{2}{3} \quad}$ $\overline{\quad 5\frac{1}{30} \quad}$ $\overline{\quad 3\frac{1}{5} \quad}$ $\overline{\quad 1\frac{9}{20} \quad}$ $\overline{\quad \frac{2}{3} \quad}$

$\overline{\quad 12\frac{11}{30} \quad}$ $\overline{\quad 11\frac{1}{3} \quad}$ $\overline{\quad 11\frac{1}{3} \quad}$ $\overline{\quad 1\frac{9}{20} \quad}$ $\overline{\quad 12\frac{11}{30} \quad}$ $\overline{\quad 3\frac{23}{24} \quad}$ $\overline{\quad 11\frac{1}{3} \quad}$ $\overline{\quad 9\frac{7}{12} \quad}$ $\overline{\quad 5\frac{1}{30} \quad}$ $\overline{\quad 3\frac{1}{5} \quad}$

What does an elf do after school?

DIRECTIONS: First, solve each of the word problems on another sheet of paper. Second, find your answer in the secret code. Third, each time your answer appears in the secret code, write the letter of the problem above it.

1. John hiked $1\frac{1}{2}$ hours on Monday, $2\frac{1}{3}$ hours on Tuesday and $1\frac{3}{4}$ hours on Wednesday. How many total hours did John hike? ____ = R

2. If a cake recipe called for $1\frac{1}{3}$ cups of flour, and Kim had only $\frac{3}{4}$ cup of flour, how much more flour did she need? ____ = M

3. If Ben's family drinks $\frac{2}{3}$ gallons of milk on Wednesday, $1\frac{3}{4}$ gallons on Thursday, $\frac{3}{4}$ gallons gallons on Friday, and $\frac{1}{2}$ gallon Saturday, how many gallons of milk did Ben's family drink in all? _____ = N

4. Gary's ant farm can hold $2\frac{1}{2}$ cups of sand. On Thursday Gary used $\frac{4}{5}$ cups of sand in his ant farm. On Friday he added $\frac{9}{10}$ cups more of sand. How much more sand will his ant farm farm hold? _____ = W

5. Robert's family made $6\frac{1}{2}$ pounds of potato salad for a community picnic. Only $3\frac{3}{4}$ pounds were eaten. How many pounds of potato salad were left? _____ = K

6. Kevin rode his bike $1\frac{1}{3}$ miles on Monday, $2\frac{5}{6}$ miles on Wednesday, and $3\frac{1}{5}$ miles on on Friday. How many total miles did he ride? ____ = E

7. Katie practiced piano for $4\frac{1}{2}$ hours during spring break. The following week she practiced $2\frac{1}{3}$ hours. How many more hours did she practice during spring break? ____ = O

8. Chris watched television for $\frac{3}{4}$ hours on Saturday, 1 hour on Monday, $1\frac{1}{2}$ hours on Tuesday, $\frac{1}{2}$ hour on Wednesday, $\frac{1}{3}$ hour on Thursday, $\frac{1}{2}$ hour on Friday, and $2\frac{1}{2}$ hours on Saturday. How many total hours did Chris watch television? ____ = G

$7\frac{1}{12}$ $3\frac{2}{3}$ $2\frac{1}{6}$ $7\frac{7}{12}$ $7\frac{11}{30}$ $\frac{4}{5}$ $2\frac{1}{6}$ $5\frac{7}{12}$ $2\frac{3}{4}$

NAME_____

What do you get when you cross an Arabian ruler and a cow?

DIRECTIONS: Solve each of the word problems below using the information given in the rainfall chart. Answers should be in the simplest form. Find your answer in the secret code. Each time your answer appears in the code, write the letter of the problem above it.

DAY	RAINFALL (in inches)
Sun.	$\frac{3}{10}$
Mon.	$\frac{1}{2}$
Tues.	none
Wed.	$\frac{1}{4}$
Thurs.	$\frac{3}{4}$
Fri.	none
Sat.	$\frac{7}{20}$

1. How many days did it rain? _____ L

2. How much more did it rain on Saturday than on Wednesday? _____ H

3. What was the Wednesday-Thursday total? _____ I

4. Thursday had the most rainfall. How much more rain fell on Thursday than on Monday? _____ K

5. Wednesday had the least amount of rainfall. How much more did it rain on Sunday than on Wednesday? _____ M

6. What was the total rainfall for the weekend? _____ E

7. What was the total rainfall for the weekdays? _____ A

8. What was the total amount of rainfall recorded on the chart? _____ S

$1\frac{1}{2}$

$\frac{1}{20}$ 1   5 $\frac{1}{4}$ $2\frac{3}{20}$ $\frac{1}{10}$ $\frac{13}{20}$ 1 $\frac{1}{4}$

Multiplying fractions with _of_

NAME_____

What did the cashier say when he was caught stealing?

DIRECTIONS: First, solve each problem below. Second, find your answer in the secret code. Third, each time your answer appears in the secret code, write the letter of the problem above it.

1. $\frac{2}{5}$ of 20 = _____(G)

2. $\frac{6}{5}$ of 10 = _____(D)

3. $\frac{7}{10}$ of an hour = _____ min. (E)

4. $\frac{3}{4}$ of a dozen = _____(H)

5. $\frac{5}{4}$ of a yard = _____ in. (W)

6. $\frac{1}{4}$ of 28 = _____(U)

7. $\frac{5}{8}$ of 16 = _____(O)

8. $\frac{2}{3}$ of a yard = _____ in. (C)

9. $\frac{3}{5}$ of an hour = _____ min. (L)

10. $\frac{4}{7}$ of 28 = _____ (M)

11. $\frac{5}{6}$ of a yard = _____ in. (A)

12. $\frac{4}{5}$ of 100 = _____(T)

13. $\frac{1}{3}$ of a foot = _____ in. (N)

14. $\frac{4}{5}$ of an hour = _____ min. (I)

| 48 | | 80 | 9 | 10 | 7 | 8 | 9 | 80 |

| 80 | 9 | 42 | | 24 | 9 | 30 | 4 | 8 | 42 |

| 45 | 10 | 7 | 36 | 12 |

| 12 | 10 | | 16 | 42 |

| 8 | 10 | 10 | 12 |

TICKLE YOUR FUNNY BONE

DIRECTIONS: First, solve each problem below on another sheet of paper. Second, find your answer in the secret code. Each time your answer appears in the secret code, write the letter of the problem above it.

1. $\dfrac{1}{3} \times \dfrac{2}{3} = $ —— (G)

2. $\dfrac{2}{5} \times \dfrac{5}{3} = $ —— (R)

3. $\dfrac{1}{2} \times \dfrac{2}{4} = $ —— (L)

4. $\dfrac{5}{6} \times \dfrac{3}{2} = $ —— (M)

5. $\dfrac{11}{12} \times \dfrac{2}{3} = $ —— (H)

6. $\dfrac{3}{7} \times \dfrac{5}{4} = $ —— (S)

7. $\dfrac{1}{4} \times \dfrac{1}{2} = $ —— (N)

8. $\dfrac{2}{3} \times \dfrac{3}{4} = $ —— (T)

9. $\dfrac{8}{9} \times \dfrac{4}{5} = $ —— (F)

10. $\dfrac{15}{16} \times \dfrac{0}{2} = $ —— (U)

11. $\dfrac{1}{9} \times \dfrac{11}{9} = $ —— (I)

12. $\dfrac{3}{5} \times \dfrac{4}{3} = $ —— (D)

13. $\dfrac{5}{6} \times \dfrac{2}{3} = $ —— (E)

14. $\dfrac{5}{8} \times \dfrac{5}{6} = $ —— (O)

VAMPIRE'S OCCUPATION:

$$\dfrac{5}{4} \quad \dfrac{25}{48} \quad \dfrac{25}{48} \quad \dfrac{1}{8} \quad \dfrac{1}{4} \quad \dfrac{11}{81} \quad \dfrac{2}{9} \quad \dfrac{11}{18} \quad \dfrac{1}{2} \quad \dfrac{11}{81} \quad \dfrac{1}{8} \quad \dfrac{2}{9}$$

MONSTER'S SWEETHEART:

$$\dfrac{11}{18} \quad \dfrac{11}{81} \quad \dfrac{15}{28} \quad \quad \dfrac{2}{9} \quad \dfrac{11}{18} \quad \dfrac{25}{48} \quad 0 \quad \dfrac{1}{4}$$

$$\dfrac{32}{45} \quad \dfrac{2}{3} \quad \dfrac{11}{81} \quad \dfrac{5}{9} \quad \dfrac{1}{8} \quad \dfrac{4}{5}$$

NAME_____

MATHOSAURUS: Who Am I?

DIRECTIONS: First, solve each problem below. Second, find your answer in the secret code. Third, each time your answer appears in the secret code, write the letter of the problem above it.

FACTS: This animal resembled a dinosaur, but it was not. It lived on Earth before the dinosaurs and was actually one of the earliest mammals. Its diet included small amphibians and reptiles. It is believed that the sail-like structure on its back was used to help regulate its body temperature and thus acted like a solar panel. This structure seized the sun's warmth, warmed the body of this mammal, and enabled it to move quickly so it could catch sluggish, sleeping prey.

1. $\frac{1}{2}$ x $\frac{3}{4}$ = —— (T)

2. $\frac{2}{3}$ x $\frac{3}{7}$ = —— (R)

3. $\frac{2}{5}$ x $\frac{7}{10}$ = —— (N)

4. $\frac{0}{4}$ x $\frac{3}{4}$ = —— (M)

5. $\frac{7}{8}$ x $\frac{2}{3}$ = —— (E)

6. $\frac{8}{9}$ x $\frac{2}{5}$ = —— (I)

7. $\frac{3}{8}$ x $\frac{1}{2}$ = —— (O)

8. $\frac{2}{3}$ x $\frac{5}{6}$ = —— (D)

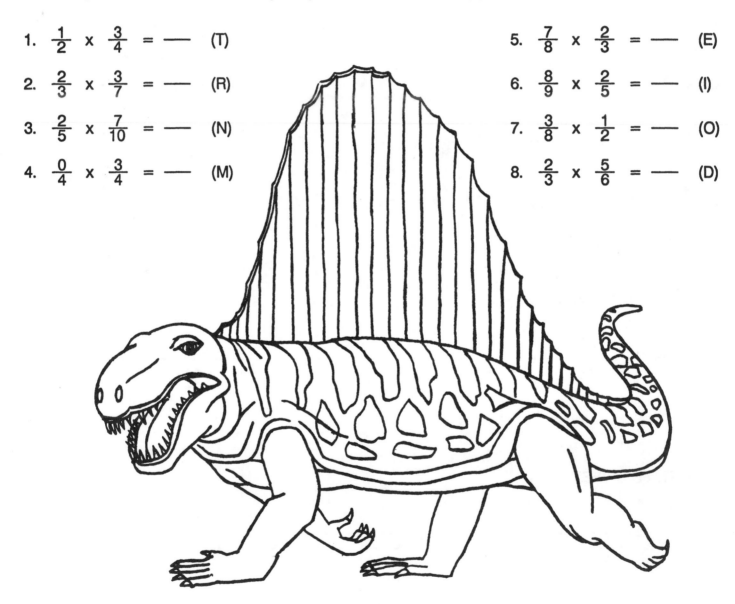

$\frac{5}{9}$ $\frac{16}{45}$ 0 $\frac{7}{12}$ $\frac{3}{8}$ $\frac{2}{7}$ $\frac{3}{16}$ $\frac{5}{9}$ $\frac{3}{16}$ $\frac{7}{25}$

NAME_____

MATH BINGO

DIRECTIONS: Work the problems and find your answer in the bingo box below. Circle the answer. When you have circled five answers in a line - horizontally, diagonally, or vertically, you have a Math Bingo.

$16\frac{5}{8}$	$67\frac{31}{32}$	$5\frac{1}{2}$	$23\frac{1}{2}$	$23\frac{11}{18}$
$27\frac{1}{3}$	6	$12\frac{1}{2}$	$4\frac{3}{29}$	$10\frac{1}{7}$
0	20	**FREE SPACE**	$5\frac{1}{4}$	$17\frac{1}{9}$
$31\frac{2}{3}$	8	$14\frac{7}{9}$	$20\frac{1}{6}$	$82\frac{1}{6}$
$9\frac{1}{3}$	$5\frac{15}{16}$	$15\frac{1}{3}$	$11\frac{3}{8}$	$6\frac{17}{18}$

1. $4\frac{3}{8} \times 1\frac{1}{5} =$ _____

2. $6\frac{1}{3} \times 5 =$ _____

3. $9\frac{3}{8} \times 7\frac{1}{4} =$ _____

4. $1\frac{2}{3} \times 4\frac{1}{6} =$ _____

5. $2\frac{1}{2} \times 2\frac{3}{8} =$ _____

6. $10 \times \frac{4}{5} =$ _____

7. $8\frac{7}{8} \times 0 =$ _____

8. $8\frac{1}{2} \times 9\frac{2}{3} =$ _____

9. $5\frac{2}{3} \times 4\frac{1}{6} =$ _____

10. $7 \times 1\frac{1}{3} =$ _____

11. $6 \times 3\frac{1}{3} =$ _____

12. $8\frac{3}{4} \times 1\frac{3}{7} =$ _____

13. $3\frac{1}{2} \times 1\frac{4}{7} =$ _____

14. $5\frac{1}{3} \times 1\frac{1}{8} =$ _____

NAME _____

Multiplying mixed numerals

What's a lazy rooster?

DIRECTIONS: First, solve each problem below on another sheet of paper. Second, find your answer in the secret code. Third, each time your answer appears in the secret code, write the letter of the problem above it.

1. $2\frac{1}{2} \times 2\frac{2}{5} =$ _____ (L)

2. $6\frac{3}{5} \times 2\frac{7}{9} =$ _____ (O)

3. $1\frac{3}{5} \times 4\frac{3}{4} =$ _____ (K)

4. $3 \times 1\frac{5}{6} =$ _____ (N)

5. $\frac{1}{3} \times 1\frac{1}{8} =$ _____ (D)

6. $8\frac{3}{4} \times 6\frac{2}{5} =$ _____ (A)

7. $4\frac{1}{6} \times 2\frac{2}{5} =$ _____ (E)

8. $6 \times \frac{2}{3} =$ _____ (C)

9. $3\frac{3}{5} \times 1\frac{1}{2} =$ _____ (T)

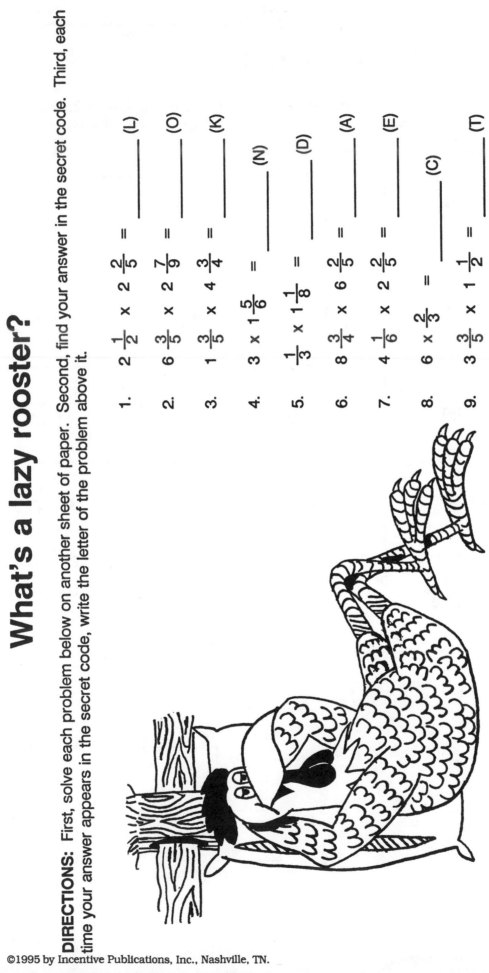

$\dfrac{}{56}$ $\dfrac{1}{4}\,18\frac{1}{3}$ $\dfrac{3}{4}\,7\frac{3}{5}$ $\dfrac{}{10}$ 6 $\dfrac{}{10}$ 6 $\dfrac{3}{8}$

$\dfrac{3}{8}\,18\frac{1}{3}$ $\dfrac{1}{5}\,5\frac{1}{2}$ $\dfrac{2}{5}\,5\frac{2}{5}$ $, \quad 18\frac{1}{3}$ $18\frac{1}{3}$ $\dfrac{3}{8}$

Why did the spy pull the sheets over his head?

DIRECTIONS: Find the reciprocal for each of the numbers in the problems below. Find your answer in the decoder and each time it occurs in the decoder, place the letter of the problem above it.

1. $\frac{1}{5}$ = _____ S

2. $\frac{19}{20}$ = _____ N

3. 16 = _____ C

4. $4\frac{1}{5}$ = _____ W

5. $\frac{5}{7}$ = _____ T

6. $17\frac{1}{2}$ = _____ H

7. 25 = _____ R

8. $12\frac{5}{8}$ = _____ G

9. $10\frac{1}{7}$ = _____ D

10. $\frac{8}{11}$ = _____ E

11. $20\frac{3}{8}$ = _____ A

12. 6 = _____ O

13. $\frac{13}{14}$ = _____ V

14. $3\frac{1}{9}$ = _____ U

$\frac{2}{35}$ $\frac{11}{8}$ $\frac{5}{21}$ $\frac{8}{163}$ $\frac{5}{1}$ $\frac{8}{163}$ $\frac{20}{19}$

$\frac{9}{28}$ $\frac{20}{19}$ $\frac{7}{71}$ $\frac{11}{8}$ $\frac{1}{25}$ $\frac{1}{16}$ $\frac{1}{6}$ $\frac{14}{13}$ $\frac{11}{8}$ $\frac{1}{25}$

$\frac{8}{163}$ $\frac{8}{101}$ $\frac{11}{8}$ $\frac{20}{19}$ $\frac{7}{5}$

NAME_____

Why is a baseball game like a pancake?

DIRECTIONS: Solve each problem, and each time your answer appears in the decoder, write the letter of the problem above it.

1. $3 \div \frac{1}{4} =$ _____ H

2. $6 \div \frac{1}{3} =$ _____ O

3. $5 \div \frac{1}{2} =$ _____ I

4. $8 \div \frac{1}{6} =$ _____ U

5. $2 \div \frac{1}{2} =$ _____ P

6. $7 \div \frac{1}{5} =$ _____ N

7. $12 \div \frac{1}{2} =$ _____ D

8. $9 \div \frac{1}{10} =$ _____ A

9. $4 \div \frac{1}{8} =$ _____ E

10. $11 \div \frac{1}{3} =$ _____ R

11. $10 \div \frac{1}{5} =$ _____ C

12. $15 \div \frac{1}{2} =$ _____ S

13. $6 \div \frac{1}{7} =$ _____ T

14. $12 \div \frac{1}{5} =$ _____ B

$\overline{60}$ $\overline{32}$ $\overline{50}$ $\overline{90}$ $\overline{48}$ $\overline{30}$ $\overline{32}$ $\overline{10}$ $\overline{42}$ $\overline{30}$

$\overline{30}$ $\overline{48}$ $\overline{50}$ $\overline{50}$ $\overline{32}$ $\overline{30}$ $\overline{30}$

$\overline{24}$ $\overline{32}$ $\overline{4}$ $\overline{32}$ $\overline{35}$ $\overline{24}$ $\overline{30}$ $\overline{18}$ $\overline{35}$

$\overline{42}$ $\overline{12}$ $\overline{32}$ $\overline{60}$ $\overline{90}$ $\overline{42}$ $\overline{42}$ $\overline{32}$ $\overline{33}$

NAME _____

Dividing simple fractions

Why was the Egyptian girl worried?

DIRECTIONS: First, solve each problem below on another sheet of paper. Second, find your answer in the secret code. Third, each time your answer appears in the secret code, write the letter of the problem above it.

1. $\dfrac{1}{5} \div \dfrac{1}{2} =$ _____ (U)

2. $\dfrac{4}{15} \div 8 =$ _____ (R)

3. $\dfrac{2}{7} \div \dfrac{1}{4} =$ _____ (H)

4. $\dfrac{9}{10} \div \dfrac{2}{5} =$ _____ (C)

5. $\dfrac{1}{10} \div \dfrac{2}{3} =$ _____ (Y)

6. $3 \div \dfrac{1}{4} =$ _____ (S)

7. $\dfrac{4}{9} \div \dfrac{8}{3} =$ _____ (E)

8. $\dfrac{2}{3} \div \dfrac{4}{7} =$ _____ (A)

9. $\dfrac{9}{5} \div 15 =$ _____ (B)

10. $\dfrac{8}{5} \div \dfrac{4}{9} =$ _____ (W)

11. $\dfrac{7}{8} \div 4 =$ _____ (M)

12. $\dfrac{7}{8} \div \dfrac{7}{4} =$ _____ (D)

Secret code:

$\dfrac{2}{5}$	$1\dfrac{1}{6}$	$2\dfrac{1}{4}$	$\dfrac{1}{6}$	$\dfrac{3}{25}$
$\dfrac{3}{20}$	$\dfrac{1}{2}$	$\dfrac{1}{30}$	$\dfrac{1}{6}$	$1\dfrac{1}{7}$
$\dfrac{1}{6}$	$1\dfrac{1}{6}$	$\dfrac{1}{2}$	$1\dfrac{1}{6}$	$\dfrac{1}{2}$
$\dfrac{1}{6}$	12	$1\dfrac{1}{6}$	$3\dfrac{3}{5}$	
$\dfrac{7}{32}$	$\dfrac{7}{32}$	$\dfrac{2}{5}$	$\dfrac{2}{5}$	$\dfrac{7}{32}$
$\dfrac{3}{20}$				

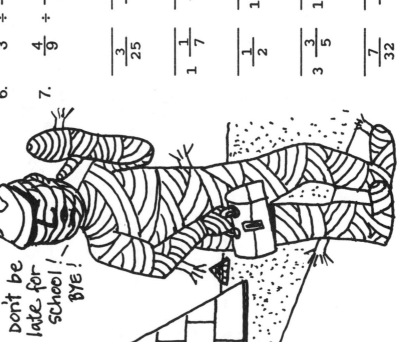

don't be late for school! — BYE!

©1995 by Incentive Publications, Inc., Nashville, TN.

Diving simple fractions

NAME _____

What's beautiful, grey and wears glass slippers?

DIRECTIONS: First, solve each problem below on another sheet of paper. Second, find your answer in the secret code. Third, each time your answer appears in the secret code, write the letter of the problem above it.

1. $\dfrac{3}{2} \div \dfrac{3}{4} =$ _____ (A)

2. $\dfrac{5}{6} \div \dfrac{4}{3} =$ _____ (T)

3. $\dfrac{1}{2} \div \dfrac{1}{3} =$ _____ (I)

4. $\dfrac{2}{3} \div 4 =$ _____ (H)

5. $\dfrac{1}{4} \div \dfrac{1}{2} =$ _____ (P)

6. $\dfrac{2}{3} \div \dfrac{3}{4} =$ _____ (L)

7. $\dfrac{3}{8} \div \dfrac{1}{2} =$ _____ (R)

8. $\dfrac{5}{6} \div \dfrac{5}{6} =$ _____ (D)

9. $\dfrac{5}{8} \div \dfrac{5}{7} =$ _____ (N)

10. $\dfrac{3}{8} \div 2 =$ _____ (E)

11. $\dfrac{5}{9} \div \dfrac{3}{2} =$ _____ (C)

$\dfrac{10}{27}$ $1\dfrac{1}{2}$ $\dfrac{7}{8}$ 1 $\dfrac{3}{16}$ $\dfrac{8}{9}$ $\dfrac{3}{16}$ $\dfrac{3}{4}$ $\dfrac{1}{2}$ $\dfrac{3}{16}$ $\dfrac{1}{6}$ 2 $\dfrac{7}{8}$ $\dfrac{5}{8}$

Dividing mixed numerals

NAME_____

Why is Dracula a great artist?

DIRECTIONS: First, solve each problem below. Second, find your answer in the secret code. Third, each time your answer appears in the secret code, write the letter of the problem above it.

1. $3\frac{1}{3} + 2\frac{1}{7}$ = _____ W

2. $8 \div 3\frac{1}{5}$ = _____ R

3. $9 \div \frac{1}{3}$ = _____ A

4. $1\frac{1}{3} \div 4$ = _____ N

5. $1\frac{3}{4} \div 4\frac{3}{8}$ = _____ O

6. $7 \div \frac{2}{3}$ = _____ E

7. $\frac{2}{3} \div 12$ = _____ L

8. $6\frac{2}{3} \div 1\frac{1}{9}$ = _____ D

9. $7 \div \frac{3}{5}$ = _____ C

10. $11 \div 2\frac{3}{4}$ = _____ H

11. $15 \div \frac{3}{4}$ = _____ B

___	___	___	___	___
4	$10\frac{1}{2}$	$11\frac{2}{3}$	27	$\frac{1}{3}$

___	___	___	___	___	___	___	___	___
6	$2\frac{1}{2}$	27	$1\frac{5}{9}$	20	$\frac{1}{18}$	$\frac{2}{5}$	$\frac{2}{5}$	6

©1995 by Incentive Publications, Inc., Nashville, TN.

NAME_____

TRIVIA: Who Am I?

DIRECTIONS: To solve the trivia puzzles, work each problem below on another sheet of paper. Find your answer in the secret code. Each time your answer appears in the secret code, write the letter of the problem above it.

1. On the day he was born, Halley's Comet was in the sky. He died seventy-five years later, the next time Halley's Comet appeared over the Earth.

2. I am an insect that lives only 2 weeks.

1. $1\frac{7}{8} \div 3\frac{1}{3} =$ _____ = W

9. $5\frac{2}{5} \div 3\frac{1}{10} =$ _____ = R

2. $3\frac{1}{7} \div 8\frac{1}{4} =$ _____ = S

10. $9 \div 2\frac{4}{7} =$ _____ = N

3. $5\frac{1}{6} \div 2\frac{7}{12} =$ _____ = Y

11. $6 \div \frac{2}{3} =$ _____ = T

4. $5\frac{2}{5} \div 1\frac{2}{7} =$ _____ = O

12. $1\frac{1}{2} \div 3\frac{2}{5} =$ _____ = E

5. $1\frac{1}{3} \div 2\frac{1}{7} =$ _____ = I

13. $8 \div \frac{1}{4} =$ _____ = K

6. $3\frac{2}{3} \div 1\frac{1}{2} =$ _____ = U

14. $2\frac{3}{8} \div 1\frac{1}{2} =$ _____ = L

7. $8 \div 3\frac{1}{5} =$ _____ = A

15. $1\frac{3}{4} \div 4\frac{3}{8} =$ _____ = M

8. $6 \div 3\frac{1}{4} =$ _____ = F

16. $5 \div \frac{4}{5} =$ _____ = H

(1) ___ ___ ___ ___   ___ ___ ___ ___ ___
$\frac{2}{5}$ $2\frac{1}{2}$ $1\frac{23}{31}$ 32 9 $\frac{9}{16}$ $2\frac{1}{2}$ $\frac{28}{45}$ $3\frac{1}{2}$

(2) ___ ___ ___ ___ ___ ___ ___ ___
$6\frac{1}{4}$ $4\frac{1}{5}$ $2\frac{4}{9}$ $\frac{8}{21}$ $\frac{15}{34}$ $1\frac{11}{13}$ $1\frac{7}{12}$ 2

Adding, subtracting, multiplying, and dividing fractions   NAME_____

Why was William Shakespeare able to write so well?

DIRECTIONS: Solve each problem, and each time your answer appears in the decoder, write the letter of the problem above it.

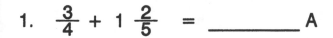

1. $\frac{3}{4} + 1\frac{2}{5} =$ _____ A

2. $2\frac{13}{20} + 4\frac{3}{5} =$ _____ E

3. $\frac{2}{3} \times \frac{3}{4} =$ _____ H

4. $9 \div \frac{1}{3} =$ _____ R

5. $2\frac{1}{2} \times 2\frac{2}{5} =$ _____ Y

6. $\frac{9}{10} \div \frac{2}{5} =$ _____ N

7. $9\frac{1}{3} \times 1\frac{9}{14} =$ _____ T

9. $8\frac{1}{4} - 5\frac{3}{7} =$ _____ I

8. $7 - 1\frac{3}{4} =$ _____ S

10. $1\frac{3}{4} \div 4\frac{3}{8} =$ _____ L

11. $4\frac{1}{3} + \frac{3}{8} + 6\frac{5}{12} + 1\frac{5}{24} =$ _____ W

$\overline{\quad}$	$\overline{\quad}$	$\overline{\quad}$	$\overline{\quad}$	$\overline{\quad}$
$12\frac{1}{3}$	$\frac{1}{2}$	$7\frac{1}{4}$	27	$7\frac{1}{4}$

$\overline{\quad}$	$\overline{\quad}$	$\overline{\quad}$	$\overline{\quad}$	$\overline{\quad}$	$\overline{\quad}$	$\overline{\quad}$
$15\frac{1}{3}$	$\frac{1}{2}$	$7\frac{1}{4}$	27	$7\frac{1}{4}$	$5\frac{1}{4}$	$2\frac{3}{20}$

'

$\overline{\quad}$	$\overline{\quad}$	$\overline{\quad}$	$\overline{\quad}$
$12\frac{1}{3}$	$2\frac{23}{28}$	$\frac{2}{5}$	$\frac{2}{5}$

'

$\overline{\quad}$	$\overline{\quad}$	$\overline{\quad}$	$\overline{\quad}$	$\overline{\quad}$	$\overline{\quad}$	$\overline{\quad}$
$15\frac{1}{3}$	$\frac{1}{2}$	$7\frac{1}{4}$	27	$7\frac{1}{4}$	$5\frac{1}{4}$	$2\frac{3}{20}$

'

$\overline{\quad}$	$\overline{\quad}$	$\overline{\quad}$
$12\frac{1}{3}$	$2\frac{3}{20}$	6

Adding, subtracting, multiplying and dividing fractions

NAME _____

What kind of music do ghosts like?

DIRECTIONS: Solve each of the problems below using the information given in the recipe. Answers should be in the simplest form. Find your answer in the secret code. Each time your answer appears in the code, write the letter of the problem above it.

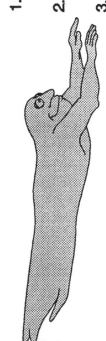

1. How many Surprise Kisses does this recipe make? _____ R

2. How many kisses are in $\frac{1}{2}$ of a recipe? _____ T

3. How much dark brown sugar would be needed for $\frac{1}{2}$ of a recipe? _____ L

4. How much oat flour would be needed for 2 recipes? _____ I

5. How much vanilla would be needed for 2 recipes? _____ U

6. How many cups of ingredients are used in the total recipe? _____ C

7. How many total teaspoons are used in the full recipe? _____ P

8. What fraction of a pound is 9 oz. of chocolate kisses? _____ S

9. How much sugar would be needed to make 9 dozen kisses? _____ A

10. Suppose that you wanted to bake a full recipe of kisses and you had only $\frac{2}{3}$ cup of flour, how much more flour will you need? _____ M

$\frac{9}{16}$	$1\frac{1}{2}$	$2\frac{1}{2}$	36	$2\frac{1}{2}$	18	1	$\frac{3}{4}$	$\frac{1}{4}$

$\frac{7}{12}$	1	$\frac{9}{16}$	$2\frac{1}{2}$	$3\frac{1}{2}$

SURPRISE KISSES
Serves 3 Dozen

$1\frac{1}{4}$ cups oat flour

1 tsp. baking soda

$\frac{1}{2}$ cup margarine

$\frac{1}{2}$ cup creamy peanut butter

$\frac{1}{2}$ cup dark brown sugar

$\frac{1}{4}$ cup sugar

$\frac{1}{2}$ tsp. vanilla

1 egg

9 oz. pkg. chocolate kisses

$\frac{1}{2}$ cup chopped pecans

DIRECTIONS: Solve each word problem below. Each time your answer occurs in the code, write the letter of that problem above it.

FACTS: I was a small meat-eating dinosaur. I was only 10 feet long and stood as tall as a man. My skeletons have been found in New Mexico and Massachusetts. Who am I?

MATHOSAURUS:

Who Am I?

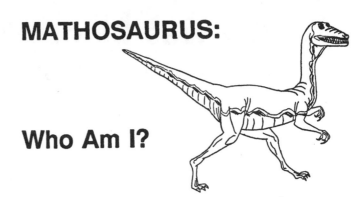

1. Tish spent $4\frac{1}{2}$ hours coaching gymnastics on Monday, $2\frac{2}{3}$ hours on Tuesday, $3\frac{1}{4}$ hours on Thursday and $2\frac{1}{2}$ hours on Friday. How many total hours did she coach?
   _____ hours (Y)

2. John took $7\frac{1}{2}$ packages of hot dog buns for the camping trip. His family used only $4\frac{1}{4}$ packages. How many packages of hot dog buns did John's family have left over? _____ (L)

3. Jack made 7 trips of $3\frac{1}{3}$ miles each to take scuba lessons. How many total miles did Jack travel? _____ (P)

4. $8\frac{3}{8}$ lbs. of blackberries were put into containers holding $1\frac{1}{4}$ lbs. each. How many containers were needed to hold the berries? _____ (H)

5. Bobby has $14\frac{2}{5}$ yards of kite string he needs to cut into 9 equal pieces. How long will each piece of string be? _____ (O)

6. Kelly needs 4 gallons of paint to paint her room. She has $2\frac{1}{2}$ gallons. How much more paint does she need? _____ (S)

7. If Gabriella's family drinks $1\frac{1}{2}$ gallons of orange juice in a week, how many gallons will they drink in 4 weeks? _____ (I)

8. Abbie spent $3\frac{1}{2}$ hours babysitting on Monday and $2\frac{3}{8}$ hours at acting class on Wednesday. How many more hours did Abbie spend babysitting than acting? _____ (E)

9. Nathan spent $1\frac{1}{2}$ hours mowing the lawn, $\frac{3}{4}$ hours cleaning his room and $1\frac{1}{3}$ hours practicing karate. How much total time did he spend on all of his activities? _____ (C)

___ ___ ___ ___ ___ ___ ___ ___ ___ ___ ___
$3\frac{7}{12}$ $1\frac{3}{5}$ $1\frac{1}{8}$ $3\frac{1}{4}$ $1\frac{3}{5}$ $23\frac{1}{3}$ $6\frac{7}{10}$ $12\frac{11}{12}$ $1\frac{1}{2}$ 6 $1\frac{1}{2}$

©1995 by Incentive Publications, Inc., Nashville, TN.

NAME_____

Why was Cinderella thrown off the baseball team?

Length Measurement
1 foot = 12 inches
1 yard = 36 inches 3 feet
1 mile = 5280 feet 1760 yards

DIRECTIONS: Solve each problem, and each time your answer appears in the decoder, write the letter of the problem above it.

1. 2 feet = _____ inches (N)

2. 5 yards = _____ feet (R)

3. 144 inches = _____ yards (S)

4. 2 miles = _____ feet (O)

5. 8½ yards = _____ inches (M)

6. 12,320 yards = _____ miles (W)

7. 216 inches = _____ feet (T)

8. 15,840 feet = _____ miles (E)

9. 15 feet = _____ yards (A)

10. 1760 yards = _____ miles (H).

11. 4½ feet = _____ inches (F)

12. 3520 yards = _____ miles (L)

13. 360 inches = _____ yards (Y)

14. 12 feet = _____ inches (B)

__	__	__	__	__	__	__	__	__	__
4	1	3	15	5	24	5	7	5	10

__	__	__	__	__	__	__	__	__	__	__
54	15	10,560	306	18	1	3	144	5	2	2

Finding examples of dozens

DOZENS, DOZENS, DOZENS

DIRECTIONS: Many items that we use everyday come in dozens. Try to think of many, varied and unusual things that come in dozens. Try to think of at least 10 examples such as cookies.

1._____

2._____

3._____

4._____

5._____

6._____

7._____

8._____

9._____

10._____

Pick one of your favorites and illustrate it.

Comparing customary units for measuring capacity

NAME_____

How does a broom act?

Capacity Measurement

1 pint: 2 cups

1 quart : 2 pints

1 gallon: 4 quarts

Directions: Solve each problem and every time your answer appears in the decoder, write the letter of the problem above it.

1. 8 quarts = _____ gallons **(T)**

2. 3 gallons = _____ quarts **(N)**

3. 8 pints = _____ gallons **(E)**

4. 2 quarts = _____ pints **(P)**

5. 2½ pints = _____ cups **(U)**

6. 6 gallons = _____ quarts **(I)**

7. 15 cups = _____ pints **(W)**

8. 1 gallon = _____ pints **(H)**

9. 3 quarts = _____ pints **(S)**

10. 4½ quarts = _____ pints **(G)**

11. 12 quarts = _____ gallons **(R)**

| 7½ | 24 | 2 | 8 | | 6 | 7½ | 1 | 1 | 4 | 24 | 12 | 9 |

| | 9 | 1 | 6 | 2 | 5 | 3 | 1 | 6 |

©1995 by Incentive Publications, Inc., Nashville, TN.

Renaming measurements as ounces, pounds, and tons

NAME_____

How many gnus are there?

Directions: Solve each problem, and each time your answer appears in the decoder, write the letter of the problem above it.

| 16 ounces = 1 lb |
| 2000 lb = 1 Ton |

1. 2 lb = _____ oz (W)

2. 80 oz = _____ lb (Y)

3. 10 T = _____ lb (O)

4. 2¾ lb = _____ oz (A)

5. 112 oz = _____ lb (D)

6. 160 oz = _____ lb (B)

7. 500 lb = _____ T (L)

8. 2 T 4 lb = _____ lb (S)

9. 5 lb 3 oz = _____ oz (N)

10. 1¼ lb = _____ oz (U)

11. 2 lb 6 oz = _____ oz (T)

12. 224 oz _____ lb (G)

| 20,000 | 83 | ¼ | 5 | 38 | 32 | 20,000 |

| 14 | 20,000 | 20,000 | 7 | 14 | 83 | 20 | 4,004 |

| 44 | 83 | 7 | 10 | 44 | 7 | 14 | 83 | 20 | 4,004 |

©1995 by Incentive Publications, Inc., Nashville, TN.

What insects were common in the time of King Arthur's Court?

Time Measurement

1 minute = 60 seconds
1 hour = 60 minutes
1 day = 24 hours
1 week = 7 days
1 year = 12 months
1 year = 52 weeks
1 year = 365 days
1 decade = 10 years
1 century = 100 years
1 millennium = 1000 years

DIRECTIONS: Solve each problem, and each time your answer appears in the decoder, write the letter of the problem above it.

1. 21 days = _____ weeks (E)

2. 3 hours = _____ minutes (U)

3. 30 months = _____ years (F)

4. $2\frac{1}{2}$ decades = _____ years (N)

5. 104 weeks = _____ years (B)

6. 3500 years = _____ millenniums (L)

7. 96 hours = _____ days (A)

8. 90 seconds = _____ minutes (S)

9. $4\frac{1}{2}$ centuries = _____ years (O)

10. 5 weeks = _____ days (R)

11. $7\frac{1}{7}$ weeks = _____ days (H)

12. 70 years = _____ decades (D)

13. 270 minutes = _____ hours (T)

14. 7 days = _____ hours (G)

| 168 | 25 | 4 | $4\frac{1}{2}$ | $1\frac{1}{2}$ | 450 | $2\frac{1}{2}$ | $4\frac{1}{2}$ | 50 | 3 |

| 35 | 450 | 180 | 25 | 7 | $4\frac{1}{2}$ | 4 | 2 | $3\frac{1}{2}$ | 3 |

NAME_____

Why is your nose in the middle of your face?

DIRECTIONS: Add or subtract these units of time. Find your answer in the decoder and each time it occurs, write the letter of the problem above it.

1. 3 hr 16 min
  + 3 hr 37 min
                = B

2. 7 min 52 s
  + 3 min 43 s
                = A

3. 6 hr 35 min
  − 4 hr 27 min
                = U

4. 7 hr 28 min
  − 2 hr 34 min
                = R

5. 5 min 13 s
  − 3 min 22 s
                = H

6. 3 hr 46 min
  + 1 hr 4 min
                = I

7. 3 hr 52 min 37 s
  + 1 hr 21 min 43 s
                = T

8. 4 h
  − 2 hr 30 min
                = E

9. 7 hr 19 min 21 s
  − 5 hr 13 min 34 s
                = N

10. 4 min 18 s
  − 2 min 11 s
                = S

11. 8 hr 2 min 30 s
  + 3 hr 12 min 42 s
                = C

―――――――   ―――――――   ―――――――――――   ―――――――   ―――――――   ―――――――   ―――――――
6 hr 53 min   1 hr 30 min   11 hr 15 min 12 sec   11 min 35 sec   2 hr 8 min   2 min 7 sec   1 hr 30 min

                              ,

―――――――   ―――――――――――   ―――――――   ―――――――――――   ―――――――   ―――――――
4 hr 50 min   5 hr 14 min 20 sec   2 min 7 sec   5 hr 14 min 20 sec   1 min 51 sec   1 hr 30 min

―――――――   ―――――――――――   ―――――――   ―――――――――   ―――――――――――   ―――――――   ―――――――
2 min 7 sec   11 hr 15 min 12 sec   1 hr 30 min   2 hr 5 min 47 sec   5 hr 14 min 20 sec   1 hr 30 min   4 hr 54 min

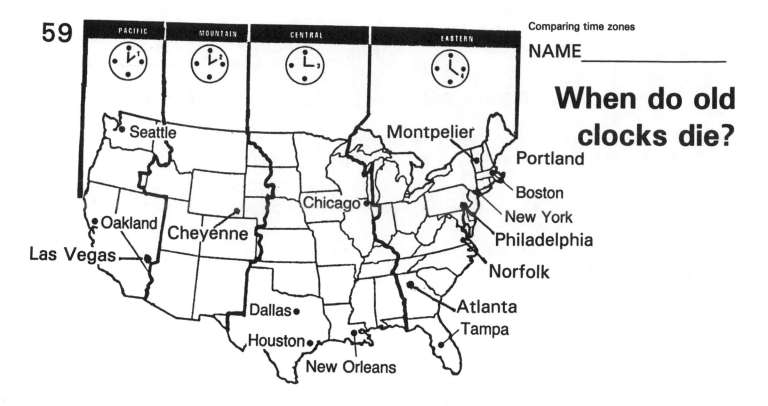

Comparing time zones

NAME_____

When do old clocks die?

Directions: Using the *United States Time Zones* map, solve each problem and each time your answer appears in the decoder, write the letter of the problem above it.

1. How many hours difference is there between Pacific and Eastern time?___(R)

2. How many hours difference between Mountain and Central time?_____(H)

3. If it is 11:00 AM in Cheyenne, Wyoming, what time is it in Norfolk, Virginia?_____(I)

4. If it is 12:00 PM in Boston, what time is it in Cheyenne, Wyoming?_____(S)

5. If you live in Montpelier, Maine and want to reach your cousin in Houston, Texas, at 7:00 PM, what time will it be in Montpelier, when you call? _____ (M)

6. If Catherine goes to bed in Seattle at 11:00 PM, what time is it in Atlanta?_____(E)

7. Jonathan lives in Oakland, CA. If he left home at 11:00 AM and returned 9½ hours later, what time did he return home?_____(N)

8. The Atlanta Braves will play baseball in Seattle at 4:30 PM. What time will the game begin on television in Atlanta?_____(P)

9. At 11:00 AM in Oakland, CA, Stacy phones her friend, Jean, in Tampa, Florida. What time is it in Tampa, when Jean answers the phone?_____(T)

10. At 9:00 AM, Jon's father left Chicago, Illinois, to drive to Philadelphia, Pennsylvania. He arrives 12 hours later. What time is it in Philadelphia when he arrives?_____(W)

11. If Lauren flies from Montpelier, Vermont, at 4:00 PM and arrives in Las Vegas, Nevada, at 6:15 PM, how long did the trip take? _____U)

10:00 PM	1	2:00 AM	8:30 PM
2:00 PM	1	2:00 AM	1:00 PM	3
2:00 PM	1:00 PM	8:00 PM	2:00 AM
1:00 PM	10:00 AM	5 hrs. 15 min	7:30 PM

©1995 by Incentive Publications, Inc., Nashville, TN.

NAME _____

What did one candle say to the other?

DIRECTIONS: First, solve each problem below on another sheet of paper. Second, find your answer in the secret code. Third, each time your answer appears in the secret code, write the letter of the problem above it.

1. $6\frac{1}{2}$ yards = _____ inches (H)

2. $3\frac{1}{2}$ miles = _____ feet (R)

3. 257 ozs. = _____ lbs. (G)

4. $7\frac{3}{4}$ hours = _____ minutes (U)

5. $8\frac{3}{5}$ years = _____ days (S)

6. 58 feet = _____ yards (T)

7. $4\frac{5}{6}$ feet = _____ inches (E)

8. $18\frac{1}{4}$ pounds = _____ ounces (O)

9. 2145 days = _____ years (L)

$16\frac{1}{16}$	3139	234	58	292
	$19\frac{1}{3}$	$19\frac{1}{3}$	58	18,480

$5\frac{64}{73}$ $16\frac{1}{16}$ 58 $19\frac{1}{3}$ $19\frac{1}{3}$

292   465 $19\frac{1}{3}$ $19\frac{1}{3}$ 292

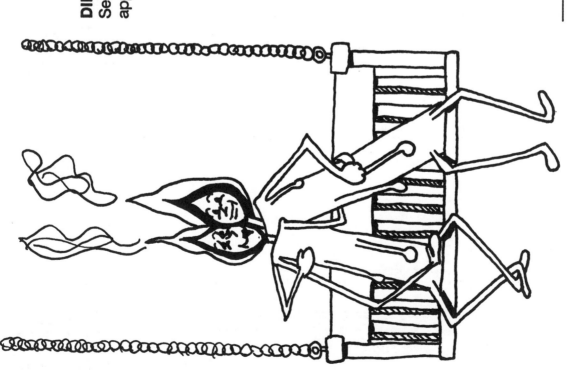

NAME_____

Which is more correct to say?
"8 + 4 is 11 or 8 + 4 are 11."

DIRECTIONS: Express each of the comparisons given below as ratios. Be careful to write your ratios in the correct order. Ratios can be written in several ways. For example, the number of trucks to sports cars can be written: 4 to 12, 4:12, or $\frac{4}{12}$. After you have written each ratio, find your answer in the decoder and write the letter of the problem above it. (Only one way of writing each ratio is given; it's up to you to discover which one!)

SPORTS CARS

TRUCKS

1. trucks to sports cars = _____ N

2. trucks to boats = _____ T

3. sports cars to boats = _____ H

4. jets to trucks = _____ 4

5. boats to trucks = _____ 8

6. air transportation to water transportation = _____ U

7. trucks to all other vehicles = _____ S

8. water transportation to land transportation = _____ R

9. jets to sports cars = _____ P

10. sports cars to all other vehicles = _____ I

11. all vehicles with wheels to those with no wheels = _____ E

12. boats to the fastest transportations = _____ L

13. all trucks to jets = _____ 12

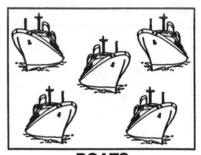

BOATS

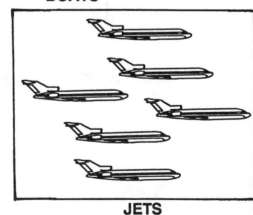

JETS

$\frac{4}{12}$ or $\frac{1}{3}$	22 to 5	12:15 or 4:5	4 out of 5	12:5	22 to 5	$\frac{5}{16}$

$\frac{5}{4}$		6 to 12 or 1 to 2	5 out of 6	6 to 5	4:23	6 to 4 or 3 to 2

12:15 or 4:5	4:23	4:6 or 2:3

Using ratios   NAME_____

RATIO SURVEY

DIRECTIONS: Complete this search by using the makeup of your class as a source for your ratios. *For example,* if there are 28 students in your class and 14 are girls and 14 are boys, you can express your ratios as: 14:28, 14 to 28, 14 out of 28, or $\frac{14}{28}$. For each question below, write your ratio in 2 different ways.

DATE OF SURVEY_____

NO. OF STUDENTS SURVEYED_____

TEACHER'S NAME_____

---

1.   Girls to boys:_____

2.   Students wearing glasses to students not wearing glasses:_____

3.   Students riding the bus to school to those who do not:_____

4.   Students with brown eyes to students with blue eyes:_____

5.   Boys to all students:_____

6.   Students not playing organized sports to those who do:_____

7.   Students who watch an average or 1 of more hours of television per day to those who watch less than an hour:_____

8.   Students playing a musical instrument to those who do not:_____

9.   Students wearing watches to those who are not:_____

10. Boys and girls to all students:_____

EXTENSION ACTIVITIES: (1) Students can design their own family questionnaire of 5 or more questions that would involve using ratios, and (2) graphs can be designed to show one or more of the results of the class survey.

Expressing unit rate

WHY DOESN'T SWEDEN EXPORT CATTLE?

DIRECTIONS: Solve each problem by writing the unit rate. Each time your answer appears in the decoder, write the letter of the problem above it. All rates are expressed in lowest terms.

1. Ken purchased 100 pencils for $4.00._____ = N

2. The Atlanta Braves paid $200.00 to have 3,000 posters printed. _____ = H

3. Catherine sold 288 magazine subscriptions in 18 days. _____ = E

4. The Grogans drove a total of 1,512 miles in 6 days._____ = L

5. A typist types 1,950 words in 30 minutes._____ = O

6. The Kodak shop processed 228 rolls of film in 4 days._____ = R

7. Furniture Crafters charges $268.15 to assemble 31 chairs._____ W

8. Cedric bought 12 pens for $1.44._____ = P

9. Bonnie's parents paid $500 for 25 lessons in horseback riding. = _____ A

10. Apples were on sale at 4 pounds for $1.20._____ = S

11. Six Flags' season tickets were on sale at 6 for $264.00_____ = K

12. The Godfreys paid $2,184 to rent a chalet for 6 months._____ C

13. Ryan sold 216 chocolate bars in 6 days for his soccer team._____ = M

14. Jean read 60 pages in 15 minutes._____ = T

1/.30	.15/1	16/1	8.65/1	$20/1	.04/1	4/1	.30/1
4/1	65/1	1/$44	16/1	16/1	.12/1	.15/1	16/1	57/1
.30/1	4/1	65/1	$364/1	1/$44	.15/1	65/1	252/1	36/1

NAME_____

Why didn't the skeleton kid want to go to school?

DIRECTIONS: Solve each problem by writing each ratio as a fraction. Each time your answer occurs in the decoder, write the letter of the problem above it.

1.   The ratio of the soccer balls to the footballs = _____ O

2.   The ratio of the baseballs to the basketballs = _____ S

3.   The ratio of the footballs to the soccer balls and baseballs = _____ A

4.   The ratio of the soccer balls to tennis balls = _____ W

5.   The ratio of basketballs to the baseballs = _____ I

6.   The ratio of soccer balls to all other balls = _____ N

7.   The ratio of footballs to soccer balls = _____ T

8.   The ratio of soccer balls to tennis balls and baseballs = _____ E

9.   The ratio of footballs to tennis balls = _____ H

10.   The ratio of tennis balls to all other balls = _____ R

$\frac{5}{10}$ or $\frac{1}{2}$ $\frac{6}{8}$ or $\frac{3}{4}$ $\frac{8}{6}$ or $\frac{4}{3}$

$\frac{5}{10}$ or $\frac{1}{2}$ $\frac{4}{18}$ or $\frac{2}{9}$ $\frac{5}{12}$ $\frac{10}{23}$ $\frac{5}{4}$

$\frac{4}{10}$ or $\frac{2}{5}$ $\frac{5}{12}$ $\frac{8}{6}$ or $\frac{4}{3}$ $\frac{4}{29}$ $\frac{4}{5}$ $\frac{5}{4}$

$\frac{6}{8}$ or $\frac{3}{4}$ $\frac{4}{29}$ $\frac{6}{8}$ or $\frac{3}{4}$ $\frac{5}{4}$

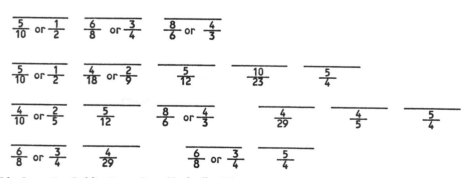

NAME_____

MARBLES AND PROBABILITY

BACKGROUND INFORMATION: To find probability, use the following ratio:

Probability of a certain outcome:	$\dfrac{\text{no. of ways a certain outcome can occur}}{\text{no. of possible outcomes}}$

For example: If there are 2 red socks, 3 blue socks, 1 black sock, and 4 green socks in a drawer in a dark room, what is the probability that you would pick a blue sock on your first try?

> The number of blue socks is 3
>
> The number of possible outcomes is ($1 + 2 + 3 + 4$ or 10)
>
> The probability that the sock will be blue is $\frac{3}{10}$

DIRECTIONS: Find the probability of each of the following if there are 5 blue marbles, 6 red marbles, 2 white marbles and 7 yellow marbles in a bag.

1. a blue marble_____

2. a white marble_____

3. a blue or white marble_____

4. a blue, white, yellow, or red marble_____

5. not a yellow or red marble_____

6. a red marble_____

7. not a yellow marble_____

8. a yellow marble_____

9. not a white marble_____

10. a green marble_____

NICKEL TOSS

NAME_____

DIRECTIONS: With a partner, you are going to toss 2 nickels simultaneously for 40 times and record your results; *but, before you do this activity*, determine the probability of these events occurring:

(1) tossing 2 heads?_____
(2) tossing 2 tails?_____
(3) tossing 1 tail and 1 head or vice versa?_____

Now, toss your coins and record your totals in the chart below. Use tally mark to group your results.

2 HEADS	2 TAILS	1 HEAD AND 1 TAIL OR VICE VERSA
Totals:_____ Fractional form: _____ Reduced fractional form:_____	Totals: _____ Fractional form:_____ Reduced fractional form:_____	Totals:_____ Fractional form:_____ Reduced fraction form:_____

Answer these questions:

1.   Did your totals match your predicted probabilities?_____If not, were any of them close? Explain._____

2.   Why do you think your totals came out the way they did?

_____

_____

Determining probability

NAME_____

WHAT ARE THE ODDS?

BACKGROUND INFORMATION: Probability can be expressed in fractional form such as:

favorable outcomes
possible outcomes

For example: If a die is thrown one time, the probability that a [⦂] will turn up is $\frac{1}{6}$.

DIRECTIONS: If a die is thrown, what is the probability of each of these events occurring? Record your responses in fractional form.

1. The number showing is a 4?_____

2. The number showing is less than 5?_____

3. The number showing is a composite number?_____

4. The number showing is a 6?_____

5. The number showing is an even number?_____

6. The number showing is a prime?_____

7. The number showing is an odd number?_____

8. The number showing is less than three?_____

9. The number showing is a multiple of 2?_____

68

Part 2 : WHAT ARE THE ODDS?

DIRECTIONS: Toss the die **60** times and record your results. Use tally marks for grouping your findings.

Number showing on your die					
1	2	3	4	5	6

Using the data from the above chart, record your findings in the chart below. Reduce all fractions to their lowest terms

	Fraction	Reduced fraction	Did it match your probability?	Was it close?
1. Number showing was a 4:	_____	_____	_____	_____
2. Number showing was less than 5:	_____	_____	_____	_____
3. Number showing was a composite no.:	_____	_____	_____	_____
4. Number showing was a 6:	_____	_____	_____	_____
5. Number showing was an even no.:	_____	_____	_____	_____
6. Number showing was a prime:	_____	_____	_____	_____
7. Number showing was an odd number:	_____	_____	_____	_____
8. Number showing is less than 3:	_____	_____	_____	_____
9. Number showing is a multiple of 2:	_____	_____	_____	_____

NAME_____

ROCK, PAPER, SCISSORS

DIRECTIONS: We can use the familiar game, *Rock, Paper, Scissors*, to enhance our understanding of how probability works. First, predict the probability of getting each of the following:

ROCK_____

PAPER_____

SCISSORS_____

With a partner, play this game 30 times and tally which position won and who won each game.

ROCK	PAPER	SCISSORS
TOTALS_____ FRACTIONAL TOTALS____ REDUCED FRACTIONAL TOTALS_____	TOTALS_____ FRACTIONAL TOTALS____ REDUCED FRACTIONAL TOTALS_____	TOTALS_____ FRACTIONAL TOTALS___ REDUCED FRACTIONAL TOTALS_____

PLAYER ONE	PLAYER TWO
NAME_____ TOTALS_____ FRACTIONAL TOTALS_____ REDUCED FRACTIONAL TOTALS_____	NAME_____ TOTALS_____ FRACTIONAL TOTALS_____ REDUCED FRACTIONAL TOTALS_____

EXTENSION ACTIVITY: CONSTRUCT A CLASSROOM GRAPH TO SHOW RESULTS.

BRAIN CHALLENGERS: FRACTIONS, RATIOS, AND PROBABILITY

NAME_____

Domino Fractions

DIRECTIONS: These dominoes represent fractions. The top half is the numerator and the bottom half is the denominator. Find the 5 dominoes that, when <u>added</u> together, equal $2\frac{2}{3}$.

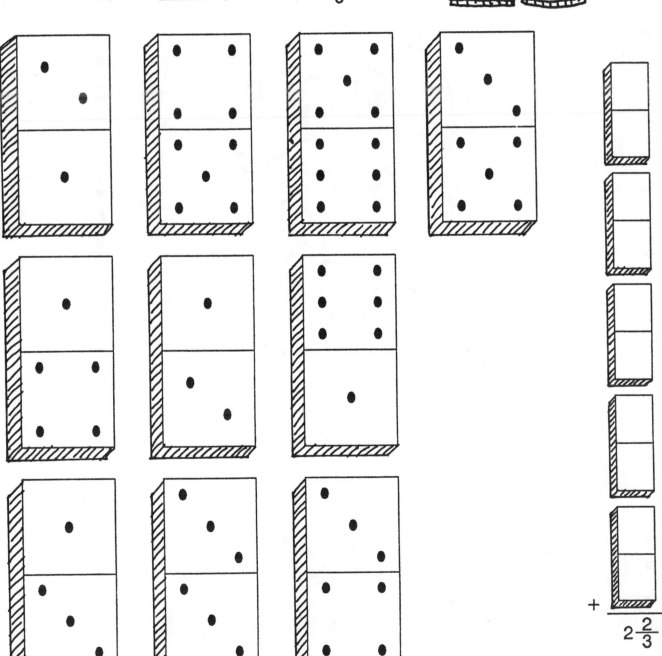

$$+ $$
$$2\frac{2}{3}$$

Application and analysis

NAME_____

Domino Fractions II

DIRECTIONS: Find the dominoes that, when <u>subtracted</u>, result in the answers given. Remember, the top half is the numerator and the bottom half is the denominator. Some problems have more than one solution, and you <u>may</u> use any domino more than once.

THINKING WORDS
arrange, rearrange
analyze, breakdown
recombine

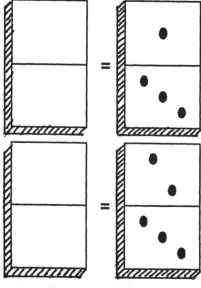

1. [ ] − [ ] = [domino]

2. [ ] − [ ] = [domino]

3. [ ] − [ ] = [domino]

4. [ ] − [ ] = [domino]

NAME_____

Combining Fractions

DIRECTIONS: Complete the addition and subtraction problems below using the fractions given at the bottom of the page.

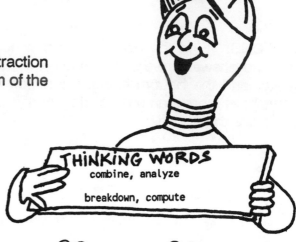

THINKING WORDS
combine, analyze

breakdown, compute

1. $\dfrac{5}{8}$ = ⬭ + ⬭

2. $\dfrac{3}{7}$ = ⬭ + ⬭

3. $\dfrac{1}{8}$ = ⬭ − ⬭

4. $\dfrac{1}{3}$ = ⬭ − ⬭

5. $\dfrac{13}{14}$ = ⬭ + ⬭

6. ⬭ + ⬭ = $\dfrac{3}{4}$

7. ⬭ + ⬭ = $\dfrac{7}{9}$

8. ⬭ − ⬭ = $\dfrac{1}{2}$

9. ⬭ − ⬭ = $\dfrac{3}{8}$

10. ⬭ − ⬭ = $\dfrac{19}{40}$

$\dfrac{3}{7}$ $\dfrac{2}{14}$ $\dfrac{2}{7}$ $\dfrac{1}{4}$ $\dfrac{3}{8}$ $\dfrac{5}{12}$ $\dfrac{7}{8}$ $\dfrac{8}{12}$

$\dfrac{1}{3}$ $\dfrac{2}{5}$ $\dfrac{1}{2}$ $\dfrac{1}{2}$ $\dfrac{13}{36}$ $\dfrac{3}{4}$ $\dfrac{2}{3}$ $\dfrac{1}{12}$

$\dfrac{3}{8}$ $\dfrac{9}{10}$ $\dfrac{2}{5}$ $\dfrac{5}{8}$

Application and analysis

NAME_____

Number Maze

DIRECTIONS: Move through this number maze as fast as
you can from start (1) to finish (2). You may move one
square in any direction, but you can only move to a number
that is either $\frac{1}{4}$ more or $\frac{1}{8}$ less than the number you are on.

Start
Here →

1	$1\frac{1}{8}$	$1\frac{7}{8}$	2	$2\frac{1}{8}$	$2\frac{3}{4}$
$\frac{7}{8}$	$\frac{5}{8}$	$1\frac{3}{8}$	$1\frac{1}{4}$	$1\frac{1}{8}$	$\frac{3}{8}$
$1\frac{1}{8}$	$1\frac{3}{4}$	1	$1\frac{1}{8}$	$1\frac{1}{2}$	$1\frac{3}{8}$
$1\frac{1}{4}$	$1\frac{3}{8}$	$1\frac{1}{4}$	$1\frac{3}{8}$	$1\frac{1}{8}$	$\frac{7}{8}$
$2\frac{7}{8}$	$1\frac{1}{2}$	$1\frac{1}{8}$	$1\frac{5}{8}$	$\frac{5}{8}$	$1\frac{1}{2}$
$1\frac{1}{8}$	$\frac{5}{8}$	$1\frac{1}{2}$	$1\frac{1}{4}$	$1\frac{7}{8}$	$1\frac{5}{8}$
$2\frac{1}{8}$	$1\frac{3}{4}$	$1\frac{7}{8}$	$1\frac{1}{8}$	2	$2\frac{1}{8}$
$1\frac{1}{4}$	2	$2\frac{1}{4}$	$1\frac{5}{8}$	$\frac{7}{8}$	$2\frac{1}{4}$
1	$1\frac{1}{2}$	$2\frac{7}{8}$	$2\frac{1}{8}$	$\frac{5}{8}$	$\frac{3}{4}$
$1\frac{1}{8}$	$\frac{5}{8}$	$1\frac{7}{8}$	2	$1\frac{5}{8}$	$1\frac{7}{8}$
$1\frac{1}{4}$	$1\frac{1}{2}$	$1\frac{1}{8}$	$1\frac{7}{8}$	$1\frac{3}{4}$	$1\frac{1}{4}$
$1\frac{1}{2}$	$\frac{3}{4}$	2	$1\frac{3}{4}$	$2\frac{1}{8}$	2

← Finish
Here

NAME_____

Number Maze II

DIRECTIONS: Move from start to finish as fast as you can!
Move one square in any direction, but you may only move to
a square $\frac{3}{4}$ more or $\frac{1}{6}$ less than the square you are on.

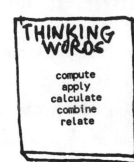

Start Here →

$\frac{3}{4}$	1	$1\frac{1}{4}$	$2\frac{3}{4}$	$2\frac{1}{4}$	3
$\frac{1}{4}$	$1\frac{1}{2}$	$1\frac{1}{6}$	$2\frac{1}{6}$	$2\frac{1}{2}$	$3\frac{1}{6}$
$1\frac{1}{3}$	$1\frac{3}{4}$	1	$2\frac{1}{2}$	$2\frac{1}{3}$	3
$1\frac{1}{6}$	$1\frac{11}{12}$	$1\frac{3}{4}$	$3\frac{1}{6}$	$2\frac{1}{6}$	$2\frac{1}{6}$
$2\frac{1}{6}$	$2\frac{1}{4}$	$2\frac{3}{4}$	3	$2\frac{11}{12}$	$3\frac{1}{6}$
$1\frac{1}{4}$	$3\frac{1}{4}$	2	$2\frac{3}{4}$	$2\frac{1}{2}$	$3\frac{1}{2}$
$2\frac{1}{4}$	$3\frac{1}{6}$	$3\frac{5}{6}$	$3\frac{1}{6}$	$4\frac{1}{4}$	$3\frac{3}{4}$
2	$2\frac{3}{4}$	$1\frac{1}{4}$	3	$2\frac{3}{4}$	$4\frac{1}{12}$
$3\frac{5}{6}$	$3\frac{1}{12}$	2	$2\frac{1}{4}$	$3\frac{1}{4}$	$4\frac{5}{6}$
$3\frac{1}{4}$	$2\frac{1}{6}$	$3\frac{1}{6}$	$2\frac{11}{12}$	$4\frac{2}{3}$	$4\frac{1}{6}$
$2\frac{1}{6}$	2	$3\frac{1}{4}$	$4\frac{1}{2}$	4	$3\frac{3}{4}$
3	$2\frac{1}{6}$	$3\frac{1}{4}$	$3\frac{5}{6}$	$4\frac{1}{3}$	$5\frac{1}{12}$

← Finish Here

Application and analysis

NAME_____

Photo Album

DIRECTIONS: Arrange these photographs without cutting them out so that all of them will fit on these three photo album pages. You will need to add, subtract, and multiply fractional numbers.

ALBUM PAGES

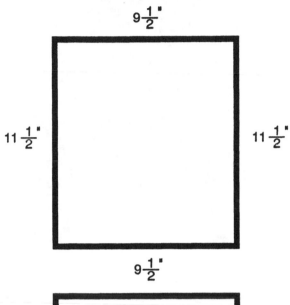

$9\frac{1}{2}"$

$11\frac{1}{2}"$ $11\frac{1}{2}"$

$9\frac{1}{2}"$

$11\frac{1}{2}"$ $11\frac{1}{2}"$

$9\frac{1}{2}"$

$11\frac{1}{2}"$ $11\frac{1}{2}"$

$9\frac{1}{2}"$

PHOTOGRAPHS

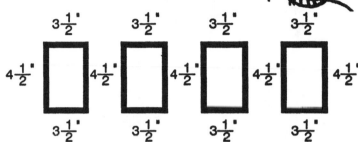

$3\frac{1}{2}"$ $3\frac{1}{2}"$ $3\frac{1}{2}"$ $3\frac{1}{2}"$

$4\frac{1}{2}"$ $4\frac{1}{2}"$ $4\frac{1}{2}"$ $4\frac{1}{2}"$ $4\frac{1}{2}"$

$3\frac{1}{2}"$ $3\frac{1}{2}"$ $3\frac{1}{2}"$ $3\frac{1}{2}"$

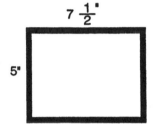 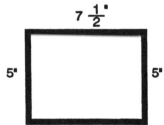

$7\frac{1}{2}"$ $7\frac{1}{2}"$

$5"$ $5"$ $5"$

$7\frac{1}{2}"$ $7\frac{1}{2}"$

 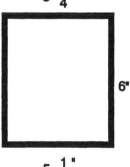

$5\frac{1}{4}"$ $5\frac{1}{4}"$

$6"$ $6"$ $6"$

$5\frac{1}{4}"$ $5\frac{1}{4}"$

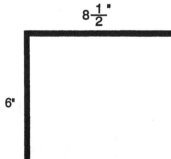

$8\frac{1}{2}"$

$6"$ $6"$

$8\frac{1}{2}"$

NAME_____

Fraction Letter Code

DIRECTIONS: Decode this message by solving the letter code and placing the correct letter of the code above the number. Only the digits 1-9 are used.

1.
$$G\frac{H}{T}$$
$$-\ H\frac{T}{T}$$
$$N\frac{T}{T}$$

2.
$$S\frac{H}{A}$$
$$-\ H\frac{T}{A}$$
$$K\frac{T}{A}$$

3.
$$T\frac{T}{H} = N\frac{N}{R}$$
$$+\ I\frac{I}{R} = I\frac{I}{R}$$
$$N\frac{S}{R}$$

4.
$$T\frac{K}{G}$$
$$+\ I$$
$$N\frac{K}{G}$$

5.
$$S\frac{K}{S}$$
$$-\ H\frac{I}{S}$$
$$K\frac{H}{S}$$

DECODING HINT: T = 1. Everywhere you see a "T", place a 1.

___ ___ ___ ___ ___ ___ ___ ___
 1   2   3   4   5   3   4   6

___ ___ ___ ___ ___ ___ ___ ___
 7   1   8   9   3   6   2   1

Analysis and application

NAME_____

Fraction Letter Code II

DIRECTIONS: To break this letter code, you must figure out what number each letter in these fraction problems represents. Only the digits 1-9 are used.

To help you, here is a hint:

Replace all <u>W</u>'s with the number <u>1</u>.

1. $\dfrac{T}{M} \times \dfrac{H}{I} = \dfrac{R}{WI}$

2. $\dfrac{P}{R} \times \dfrac{M}{H} = \dfrac{TW}{MI}$

3. $\dfrac{W}{A} \div \dfrac{W}{T} = \dfrac{T}{A}$ or $\dfrac{W}{M}$

4. $\dfrac{H}{S} \div \dfrac{W}{M} = \dfrac{WT}{S}$ or $W\dfrac{W}{M}$

5. $\dfrac{W}{R} \times \dfrac{W}{A} = \dfrac{W}{HR}$

$$\overline{9}\ \overline{3}\ \overline{6}\ \overline{8}\ \overline{2}\qquad \overline{6}\ \overline{9}\qquad \overline{6}$$

$$\overline{1}\ \overline{4}\ \overline{5}\ \overline{7}$$

NAME_____

Fractional Parts

1. **DIRECTIONS:** In this rectangular prism, first determine how many small cubes are in the whole prism. Then determine what <u>fractional</u> part of the whole prism the following are:

a) number of cubes in prism _____

b) number of cubes with dots 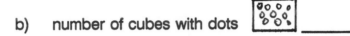 _____

c) number of cubes with diagonal lines 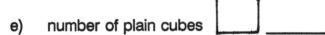 _____

d) number of cubes with cross lines _____

e) number of plain cubes  _____

2. **DIRECTIONS:** In this pyramid determine how many triangles there are on the surface of the <u>whole</u> pyramid. Then determine what <u>fractional</u> part the following are:

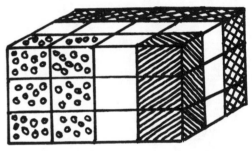

a) number of triangles on pyramid _____

b) number of triangles with dots  _____

c) number of triangles with horizontal and vertical lines 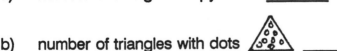 _____

d) number of plain triangles  _____

e) number of triangles with diagonal lines  _____

NAME_____

Fraction Box

DIRECTIONS: Examine the fraction box and complete the equations by using the information in the box. Two have <u>been done</u> for you.

combine, breakdown

calculate, relate

differentiate

A = $\frac{1}{4}$ of 1 = $\frac{1}{4}$

B = $\frac{1}{2}$ of $\frac{1}{4}$ = $\frac{1}{8}$

C = _____ of _____ = _____

D = _____ of _____ = _____

1. = _____ of _____ = _____

2. = _____ of _____ = _____

E = _____ of _____ = _____

F = _____ of _____ = _____

G = _____ of _____ = _____

H = _____ of _____ = _____

3. = _____ of _____ = _____

4. = _____ of _____ = _____

A	**B**
	C **D** / **D**
E E 1.___ **E E 2.___** **G G** **G G 3.___** **G G** **G I I**	**F** **H** **4.___**

combine
breakdown
calculate
differentiate
relate

Super Challenge: Fraction Box II

DIRECTIONS: Examine the fraction box and complete the equations by using the information in the box. Two have been done for you.

A = $\frac{1}{2}$ of $\frac{1}{4}$ = $\frac{1}{8}$

B = $\frac{3}{4}$ of $\frac{1}{4}$ = $\frac{3}{16}$

C = _____ of _____ = _____

D = _____ of _____ = _____

E = _____ of _____ = _____

F = _____ of _____ = _____

G = _____ of _____ = _____

H = _____ of _____ of _____ = _____

I = _____ of _____ of _____ = _____

J = _____ of _____ of _____ = _____

K = _____ of _____ = _____

L = _____ of _____ = _____

M = _____ of _____ of _____ = _____

N = _____ of _____ of _____ = _____

A		B	B
D	D		
D	D	C	B
E	G	G	L
F	G	G	L
F	G	K	L
H	I / J	K	K	M / N

Analysis and application

NAME_____

The Birthday Party

DIRECTIONS: Mrs. Johnson wanted to invite 25 people to Jane's birthday party (including Jane). If she planned to serve both cake and blueberry muffins, how much of the following items would she have to buy?

flour _____ cups

oil _____ cups

sugar _____ cups

blueberries _____ cups

eggs _____

coconut _____ cups

Blueberry Muffins (serves 5)
$1\frac{1}{2}$ c. flour
2 eggs
$\frac{3}{4}$ c. sugar
$\frac{1}{4}$ c. oil
1 cup blueberries

Coconut Cake (serves 10)
$3\frac{1}{4}$ c. flour
3 eggs
$1\frac{1}{2}$ c. sugar
$\frac{2}{3}$ c. oil
$\frac{1}{2}$ c. coconut

NAME_____

Symbol Fractions

DIRECTIONS: If the following symbols represent the fractions below, complete the chart with the correct symbols. An example has been done for you. (Answers may vary.)

$$\frac{1}{2} = \oplus \qquad \frac{1}{3} = \wedge \qquad \frac{1}{4} = \amalg$$

$$\frac{1}{6} = \diamondsuit \qquad \frac{2}{3} = \triangle \qquad \frac{3}{4} = \exists$$

Example:

$$\frac{1}{2} = \boxed{\amalg} + \boxed{\amalg}$$
$$\left(\frac{1}{4} + \frac{1}{4} = \frac{1}{2} \right)$$

1. $\frac{5}{6}$ = ☐ + ☐

2. $\frac{3}{4}$ = ☐ + ☐

3. $\frac{1}{2}$ = ☐ − ☐

4. $\frac{7}{12}$ = ☐ + ☐

5. 1 = ☐ + ☐

6. $1\frac{1}{12}$ = ☐ + ☐

7. $\frac{1}{3}$ = ☐ − ☐

8. $\frac{5}{12}$ = ☐ − ☐

9. $1\frac{1}{6}$ = ☐ + ☐

10. $\frac{1}{6}$ = ☐ − ☐

Application and analysis

NAME_____

Matching Ratios to Form Proportions

DIRECTIONS: An equation stating that two ratios are equivalent is called a <u>proportion</u>. Match the following ratios so that each one forms a proportion.

HINT: By cross multiplying, you can check two ratios.

$\frac{6}{4}$ **X** $\frac{21}{14}$ 6 x 14 = 84   These ratios <u>do</u>
                      4 x 21 = 84   form a proportion.

MATCHING:

_____ 1. $\frac{3}{7}$ A. $\frac{42}{24}$

_____ 2. $\frac{2}{5}$ B. $\frac{8}{12}$

_____ 3. $\frac{7}{21}$ C. $\frac{14}{35}$

_____ 4. $\frac{4}{7}$ D. $\frac{8}{2}$

_____ 5. $\frac{6}{12}$ E. $\frac{24}{42}$

_____ 6. $\frac{2}{3}$ F. $\frac{16}{2}$

_____ 7. $\frac{7}{4}$ G. $\frac{7}{14}$

_____ 8. $\frac{24}{3}$ H. $\frac{21}{49}$

_____ 9. $\frac{12}{3}$ I. $\frac{12}{15}$

_____ 10. $\frac{4}{5}$ J. $\frac{1}{3}$

NAME_____

Using Ratios to Save Money

DIRECTIONS: Good shoppers can use ratios to make sure they are getting the best buys. By using this simple formula of different sizes and prices, find out which will save them money.

Item 1		Item 2
$\dfrac{\text{Price of 1}}{\text{Size of 1}}$	**X**	$\dfrac{\text{Price of 2}}{\text{Size of 2}}$

(cross multiply)

Price 1 x Size 2   Price 2 x Size 1

Example: 2 loaves of bread. Loaf 1 is 20 ounces for 87¢ and Loaf 2 is 16 ounces for 68¢.

$$\frac{87}{20} \ \textbf{X} \ \frac{68}{16}$$

(cross multiply)

87 x 16   68 x 20

1392   1360

↑ smaller number, so loaf <u>2</u> is better buy.

One more example:

5 pieces of candy for 37¢

6 pieces of candy for 42¢

$$\frac{37}{5} \ \textbf{X} \ \frac{42}{6}$$

37 x 6   42 x 5

222   210

↑ 6 pieces of candy for 42¢ is better buy.

Decide which of the following items is the better buy:

1. a) 3 ounces cheese for $2.00
    b) 4 ounces cheese for $3.00

2. a) 8 ounces meat for $7.00
    b) 6 ounces meat for $5.00

3. a) 10 ounces ham for $3.50
    b) 9 ounces ham for $3.10

4. a) 5 eggs for 70¢
    b) 6 eggs for 80¢

5. a) 13 apples for $.160
    b) 14 apples for $1.75

6. a) 3 pounds hamburger for $4.75
    b) 5 pounds hamburger for $6.00

7. a) 2 pounds carrots for $1.29
    b) 5 pounds carrots for $3.00

8. a) 12 ounces shampoo for $2.95
    b) 15 ounces shampoo for $3.25

Determining probability

NAME_____

52 CARD PROBABILITY

BACKGROUND INFORMATION: In a standard deck of playing cards there, are 52 cards. There are four different suites: hearts, clubs, diamonds, and spades. Hearts and diamonds are red; clubs and spades are black. In each suit, cards are numbered 2-10 plus a jack, queen, king, and ace. Therefore, there are 13 hearts, 13 clubs, 13 diamonds, and 13 spades in every deck of cards. This also means there are 26 red cards and 26 black cards.

DIRECTIONS: Using this information, find the probability of drawing these cards at random. The first one has been done for you.

1. the ace of spades $\frac{1}{52}$

2. a red card _____

3. a queen _____

4. a heart or a diamond _____

5. an ace or a king _____

6. not a club _____

7. a seven, eight or nine _____

8. a red or black card _____

9. not a face card _____

10. the jack of hearts_____

11. the queen of diamonds _____

12. not a red or black card _____

13. a two, three, four, or five _____

14. the two of clubs _____

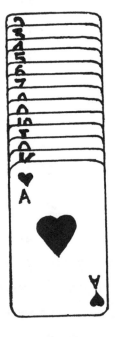

©1995 by Incentive Publications, Inc., Nashville, TN.

87

ANSWER KEY

1. Where in the World? Answers will vary.

2. The Case of the Numerator and Denominator   Answers will vary.

3. What happens to a thief if he falls into a cement mixer? —HE BECOMES A HARDENED CRIMINAL

4. **FACTORS**
   1. 18 = 1, 2, 3, 6, 9, 18
   2. 16 = 1, 2, 4, 8, 16
   3. 24 = 1, 2, 3, 4, 6, 8, 12, 24
   4. 30 = 1, 2, 3, 5, 6, 10, 15, 30
   5. 12 = 1, 2, 3, 4, 6, 12
   6. 32 = 1, 2, 4, 8, 16, 32
   7. 60 = 1, 2, 3, 4, 5, 6, 10, 12, 15, 20, 30, 60
   8. 35 = 1, 5, 7, 35

   9. 6
   10. 2
   11. 12
   12. 15
   13. 4

   14. 2
   15. 8
   16. 30
   17. 6
   18. 5

   Final answer = <u>90</u>

5. What does the invisible man drink at snack time?—EVAPORATED MILK

6. Who are the slowest talkers in the whole world?—CONVICTS - THEY SPEND 25 YEARS ON A SINGLE SENTENCE

7. The Sieve of Erathosthenes - Primes less than 100: 2, 3, 5, 7, 11, 13, 17, 19, 23, 29, 31, 37, 41, 43, 47, 53, 59, 61, 67, 73, 79, 83, 89, 97

8. **PRIME SEARCH**
   1. 25   2. 1-2   3. 1-97   4. Column 3   5. Columns 2 and 5   6. 2-83, 89   7. Rows 1 and 2
   8. Columns 1 and 9   9. 6 pairs - 5,7; 17,19; 29,31; 41,43; 59,61; 71,73   10. Row 10-97

9. **PRIME OR COMPOSITE:**
   1. Prime 2. Prime 3. Composite 4. Prime 5. Composite 6. Prime 7. Composite 8. Composite 9. Composite
   10. Prime 11. Composite 12. Prime 13. Composite 14. Composite 15. Composite 16. Prime 17. Composite
   18. Prime 19. Composite 20. Composite 21. Composite 22. Prime 23. Composite 24. Composite

10. **FACTOR TREES**
    1. 12 = 2 x 3 x 2   2. 16 = 2 x 2 x 2 x 2   3. 30 = 5 x 2 x 3   4. 36 = 2 x 3 x 2 x 3
    5. 45 = 3 x 5 x 3   6. 50 = 2 x 5 x 5   7. 72 = 2 x 2 x 2 x 3 x 3   8. 75 = 3 x 5 x 5

11. **FACTOR TREES**
    1. 56 = 7 x 2 x 2 x 2   2. 70 = 7 x 5 x 2   3. 48 = 2 x 2 x 3 x 2 x   4. 90 = 3 x 5 x 3 x 2
    5. 100 = 5 x 5 x 2 x 2   6. 64 = 2 x 2 x 2 x 2 x 2 x 2   7. 28 = 7 x 2 x 2   8. 63 = 3 x 3 x 7

12. **PRIME FACTORIZATION**
    1. 42 = 2 x 3 x 7   2. 33 = 3 x 11   3. 36 = 3 x 3 x 2 x 2   4. 72 = 2 x 2 x x 2 x 3 x 3
    5. 48 = 2 x 3 x 2 x 2 x 2   6. 50 = 2 x 5 x 5   7. 45 = 3 x 5 x 3   8. 64 = 2 x 2 x 2 x 2 x 2 x 2
    9. 81 = 3 x 3 x 3 x 3   10. 20 = 5 x 2 x 2   11. 100 = 5 x 2 x 5 x 2

13. **USING THE SLIDE**
    1. 5, 15, $\frac{1}{3}$ 2. 3, 24, $\frac{1}{8}$ 3. 3, 165, $\frac{5}{11}$ 4. 4, 40, $\frac{2}{5}$ 5. 9, 90, $\frac{2}{5}$ 6. 8, 80, $\frac{2}{5}$
    7. 1, 555, $\frac{15}{37}$ 8. 14, 18, $\frac{2}{3}$ 9. 7, 98, $\frac{2}{7}$ 10. 7, 70, $\frac{2}{5}$ 11. 5, 105, $\frac{3}{7}$ 12. 11, 66, $\frac{2}{3}$
    13. 5, 75, $\frac{3}{5}$ 14. 3, 60, $\frac{4}{5}$ 15. 4, 80, $\frac{4}{5}$ 16. 1, 2812, $\frac{37}{76}$ 17. 7, 441, $\frac{7}{9}$ 18. 2, 3900, $\frac{39}{50}$

14. **ANTICS** — What aardvarks like on their pizza: ANTCHOVIES
    What aardvarks take for an upset stomach: ANTACIDS
    Where aardvarks go to ski: ANTARCTICA

15. **CHOCOLATE DELIGHT**

    $\frac{1}{4} = \frac{3}{12}$ $\frac{3}{6} = \frac{6}{12}$ $\frac{5}{6} = \frac{10}{12}$ $\frac{3}{4} = \frac{9}{12}$ $\frac{6}{6} = \frac{12}{12}$ $\frac{2}{3} = \frac{8}{12}$

    $\frac{2}{6} = \frac{4}{12}$ $\frac{2}{4} = \frac{6}{12}$ $\frac{4}{6} = \frac{8}{12}$ $\frac{1}{3} = \frac{4}{12}$ $\frac{1}{6} = \frac{2}{12}$ $\frac{1}{2} = \frac{6}{12}$

16. Why didn't the skeleton cross the road? — BECAUSE IT DIDN'T HAVE ANY GUTS

17. What does a worm do in a corn field? —-HE GOES IN ONE EAR AND OUT THE OTHER

18. Why did Humpty Dumpty have a great fall? — TO MAKE UP FOR HIS MISERABLE SUMMER

19. What did Mrs. Claus say to her husband during the rainstorm? —COME AND LOOK AT THE REINDEER

20. Why did the umpire throw the chicken out of the game? — HE SUSPECTED FOWL PLAY

21. GHOULISH DEFINITIONS — Q - A vampire's dog
    A - A BLOODHOUND
    Q - A witch's purse
    A - A HAGBAG

22. DAFFY DEFINITIONS — Q. - Metric Cookie
    A. - A GRAM CRACKER
    Q. - Declaration of Independence
    A. - A NOTE EXCUSING YOU FROM SCHOOL

23. PHOBIAS!   PHOBIAS!   PHOBIAS!   Q. - Acrophobia
    A. - FEAR OF HEIGHTS
    Q. - Triskaidekaphobia
    A. - FEAR OF THE NUMBER THIRTEEN

24. How many months have 28 days? — ALL THE MONTHS DO

25. What happens when the frog's car breaks down? — HE GETS TOAD AWAY

26. Why did the astronaut take a shovel into space? — TO DIG A BLACK HOLE

27. Why is six afraid of seven? — BECAUSE SEVEN ATE NINE

28. Why did the Cyclops have to close his school? — BECAUSE HE HAD ONLY ONE PUPIL

29. What's the only thing to eat on a deserted island? — ONLY THE SAND WHICH IS THERE

30. What is the nationality of Santa Claus? — HE IS NORTH POLISH

31. Where is the only place in the world an elephant can visit the dentist? — TUSCALOOSA, ALABAMA

32. Where is the coldest place in the theater? — IN Z ROW

33. What's grey, heavy and sends people to sleep? — A HYPNOPOTAMUS

34. How do Martian cowboys greet each other? — WITH COMMUNICATION SADDLELIGHTS

35. What meal did the Revolutionists serve to catch spies? — CHICKEN CATCH A TORY

36. What did one magnet say to the other magnet? — I FIND YOU VERY ATTRACTIVE

37. What does an elf do after school? — GNOMEWORK

38. What do you get when you cross an Arabian ruler and a cow? — A MILKSHEIK

39. What did the cashier say when he was caught stealing? — I THOUGHT THE CHANGE WOULD DO ME GOOD

40. TICKLE YOUR FUNNY BONE — Q. - Vampire's Occupation
    A. - MOONLIGHTING
    Q - Monster's Sweetheart
    A. -HIS GHOULFRIEND

41. MATHOSAURUS: Who Am I? — DIMETRODON

42. MATH BINGO
    SECOND COLUMN: $67\frac{31}{32}$, 6, 20, 8, $5\frac{15}{16}$

43. What's a lazy rooster? — A COCK-A-DODDLE DON'T

44. Why did the spy put the sheets over his head? — HE WAS AN UNDERCOVER AGENT

45. Why is baseball like a pancake? — BECAUSE ITS SUCCESS DEPENDS ON THE BATTER

46. Why was the Egyptian girl worried? — BECAUSE HER DADDY WAS A MUMMY

47. What's beautiful, grey, and wears glass slippers? — CINDERELEPHANT

48. Why is Dracula a great artist? — HE CAN DRAW BLOOD

49. TRIVIA: Who Am I? —   (I) - MARK TWAIN   (2) - HOUSEFLY

50. Why was William Shakespeare able to write so well? — WHERE THERE'S A WILL, THERE'S A WAY

51. What kind of music do ghosts like? — SPIRITUAL MUSIC

52. MATHOSAURUS: Who Am I? — COELOPHYSIS (seel-oh-fy-sis)

53. Why was Cinderella thrown off the baseball team? —SHE RAN AWAY FROM THE BALL

54. Dozens, Dozens, Dozens - Answers will vary.

89

55. How does a broom act? — WITH SWEEPING GESTURES

56. How many kinds of gnus are there? —ONLY TWO: GOOD GNUS AND BAD GNUS

57. What insects were common in the time of King Arthur's court? —GNATS OF THE ROUND TABLE

58. Why is your nose in the middle of your face? —BECAUSE IT'S THE SCENTER

59. When do old clocks die? — WHEN THEIR TIME IS UP

60. What did one candle say to the other? — LET'S GO OUT TOGETHER

61. Which is more correct to say, 8 = 4 _is_ 11 or 8 = 4 _are_ 11? — NEITHER, 8 PLUS 4 IS 12

62. Ratio Survey - Answers will vary.

63. Why doesn't Sweden export cattle? —SHE WANTS TO KEEP HER STOCKHOLM

64. Why didn't the skeleton kid want to go to school? — HIS HEART WAS NOT IN IT

65. **MARBLES AND PROBABILITY**

1. $\frac{5}{20}$ or $\frac{1}{4}$ 2. $\frac{2}{20}$ or $\frac{1}{10}$ 3. $\frac{7}{20}$ 4. $\frac{20}{20}$ or 1   5. $\frac{7}{20}$

6. $\frac{6}{20}$ or $\frac{3}{10}$ 7. $\frac{13}{20}$ 8. $\frac{7}{20}$ 9. $\frac{18}{20}$ or $\frac{9}{10}$ 10. $\frac{0}{20}$ or 0

66. **NICKEL TOSS**

(1) $\frac{1}{4}$ or 1 out of 4   (2) $\frac{1}{4}$ or 1 out of 4   (3) $\frac{2}{4}$ or $\frac{1}{2}$ or 1 out of 2

67-68. **WHAT ARE THE ODDS?**

1. $\frac{1}{6}$ 2. $\frac{4}{6}$ or $\frac{2}{3}$ 3. $\frac{2}{6}$ or $\frac{1}{3}$ 4. $\frac{1}{6}$ 5. $\frac{3}{6}$ or $\frac{1}{2}$ 6. $\frac{3}{6}$ or $\frac{1}{2}$

7. $\frac{3}{6}$ or $\frac{1}{2}$ 8. $\frac{2}{6}$ or $\frac{1}{3}$ 9. $\frac{3}{6}$ or $\frac{1}{2}$

69. **ROCK, PAPER, SCISSORS**

Rock = $\frac{1}{3}$ Paper = $\frac{1}{3}$ Scissors = $\frac{1}{3}$

71. **DOMINO FRACTIONS**

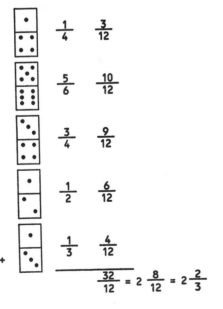

$\frac{1}{4}$ $\frac{3}{12}$

$\frac{5}{6}$ $\frac{10}{12}$

$\frac{3}{4}$ $\frac{9}{12}$

$\frac{1}{2}$ $\frac{6}{12}$

$\frac{1}{3}$ $\frac{4}{12}$

$\frac{32}{12} = 2\frac{8}{12} = 2\frac{2}{3}$

72. **DOMINO FRACTIONS I I**

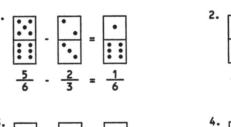

1. $\frac{5}{6} - \frac{2}{3} = \frac{1}{6}$ 2. $\frac{2}{3} - \frac{1}{3} = \frac{1}{3}$

3. $\frac{1}{2} - \frac{1}{4} = \frac{1}{4}$ 4. $\frac{5}{6} - \frac{1}{6} = \frac{2}{3}$

73. **COMBINING FRACTIONS**

1. $\frac{5}{8} = \frac{1}{4} + \frac{3}{8}$ 2. $\frac{3}{7} = \frac{2}{7} + \frac{2}{14}$ 3. $\frac{1}{8} = \frac{5}{8} - \frac{1}{2}$ 4. $\frac{1}{3} = \frac{8}{12} - \frac{1}{3}$ 5. $\frac{13}{14} = \frac{3}{7} + \frac{1}{2}$

6. $\frac{2}{3} + \frac{1}{12} = \frac{3}{4}$ 7. $\frac{13}{36} + \frac{5}{12} = \frac{7}{9}$ 8. $\frac{9}{10} - \frac{2}{5} = \frac{1}{2}$ 9. $\frac{3}{4} - \frac{3}{8} = \frac{3}{8}$ 10. $\frac{7}{8} - \frac{2}{5} = \frac{19}{40}$

74.   NUMBER MAZE

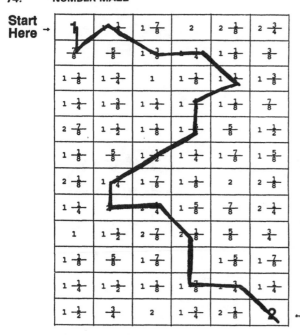

Start Here →   Finish Here ←

75.   NUMBER MAZE II

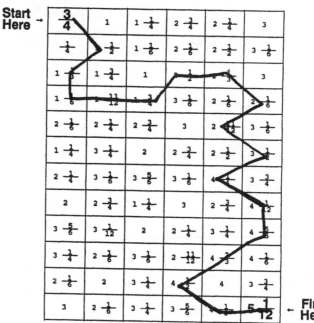

Start Here →   Finish Here ←

76.   PHOTO ALBUM

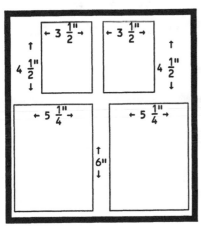

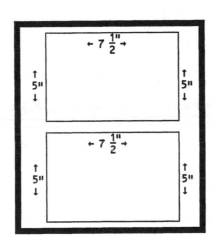

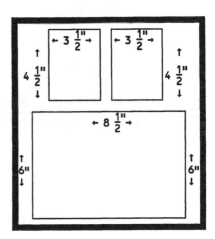

77.   FRACTION LETTER CODE

1. $6\frac{2}{3}$
  $-2\frac{1}{3}$
  $4\frac{1}{3}$

2. $7\frac{2}{9}$
  $-2\frac{1}{9}$
  $5\frac{1}{9}$

3. $1\frac{1}{2} = \frac{4}{8}$
  $+3\frac{3}{8} = \frac{3}{8}$
  $4\frac{7}{8}$

4. $7\frac{5}{6}$
  -3
  $4\frac{5}{6}$

5. $7\frac{5}{7}$
  $-2\frac{3}{7}$
  $5\frac{2}{7}$

78.   FRACTION LETTER CODE II

1. $\frac{2}{3} \times \frac{4}{5} = \frac{8}{15}$

2. $\frac{7}{8} \times \frac{3}{4} = \frac{21}{32}$

3. $\frac{1}{6} \div \frac{1}{2} = \frac{2}{6} = \frac{1}{3}$

4. $\frac{4}{9} \div \frac{1}{3} = \frac{12}{9} = 1\frac{1}{3}$

5. $\frac{1}{8} \times \frac{1}{6} = \frac{1}{48}$

©1995 by Incentive Publications, Inc., Nashville, TN.

79. FRACTIONAL PARTS

1. a) 36
   b) $\frac{6}{36}$ or $\frac{1}{6}$
   c) $\frac{3}{36}$ or $\frac{1}{12}$
   d) $\frac{12}{30}$ or $\frac{1}{3}$
   e) $\frac{15}{36}$ or $\frac{5}{12}$

2. a) 64
   b) $\frac{4}{64}$ or $\frac{1}{16}$
   c) $\frac{12}{64}$ or $\frac{3}{16}$
   d) $\frac{20}{64}$ or $\frac{5}{16}$
   e) $\frac{28}{64}$ or $\frac{7}{16}$

80. FRACTION BOX

$A = \frac{1}{4}$ of $1 = \frac{1}{4}$

$B = \frac{1}{2}$ of $\frac{1}{4} = \frac{1}{8}$

$C = \frac{1}{4}$ of $\frac{1}{4} = \frac{1}{16}$

$D = \frac{1}{2}$ of $\frac{1}{16} = \frac{1}{32}$

$E = \frac{1}{4}$ of $\frac{1}{16} = \frac{1}{64}$

$F = \frac{3}{4}$ of $\frac{1}{4} = \frac{3}{16}$

$G = \frac{1}{4}$ of $\frac{1}{32} = \frac{1}{128}$

$H = \frac{3}{4}$ of $\frac{1}{16} = \frac{3}{64}$

$I = \frac{1}{2}$ of $\frac{1}{128} = \frac{1}{256}$

$1 = \frac{1}{2}$ of $\frac{1}{16} = \frac{1}{32}$

$2 = \frac{1}{2}$ of $\frac{1}{16} = \frac{1}{32}$

$3 = \frac{1}{4}$ of $\frac{1}{4} = \frac{1}{16}$

$4 = \frac{1}{4}$ of $\frac{1}{16} = \frac{1}{64}$

81. FRACTION BOX II

$A = \frac{1}{2}$ of $\frac{1}{4} = \frac{1}{8}$

$B = \frac{3}{4}$ of $\frac{1}{4} = \frac{3}{16}$

$C = \frac{1}{4}$ of $\frac{1}{4} = \frac{1}{16}$

$D = \frac{4}{8} \left(\frac{1}{2}\right)$ of $\frac{1}{4} = \frac{1}{8}$

$E = \frac{1}{8}$ of $\frac{1}{4} = \frac{1}{32}$

$F = \frac{2}{8} \left(\frac{1}{4}\right)$ of $\frac{1}{4} = \frac{1}{16}$

$G = \frac{5}{8}$ of $\frac{1}{4} = \frac{5}{32}$

$H = \frac{1}{2}$ of $\frac{1}{8}$ of $\frac{1}{4} = \frac{1}{64}$

$I = \frac{1}{2}$ of $\frac{1}{16} \left(\frac{1}{2} \text{ of } \frac{1}{8}\right)$ of $\frac{1}{4} = \frac{1}{128}$

$J = \frac{1}{2}$ of $\frac{1}{32} \left(\frac{1}{2} \text{ of } \frac{1}{16}\right)$ of $\frac{1}{4} = \frac{1}{256}$

$K = \frac{3}{8}$ of $\frac{1}{4} = \frac{3}{32}$

$L = \frac{3}{8}$ of $\frac{1}{4} = \frac{3}{32}$

$M = \frac{1}{2}$ of $\frac{1}{8}$ of $\frac{1}{4} = \frac{1}{64}$

$N = \frac{1}{4}$ of $\frac{1}{8}$ of $\frac{1}{4} = \frac{1}{128}$

82. BIRTHDAY PARTY

flour = $15 \frac{5}{8}$ cups

sugar = $7 \frac{1}{2}$ cups

eggs = 18

oil = $2 \frac{11}{12}$ cups

blueberries = 5 cans

coconut = $1 \frac{1}{4}$ cups

83. SYMBOL FRACTIONS (Answers may vary)

1. $\frac{5}{6} = \triangle + \Diamond$

2. $\frac{3}{4} = \oplus + \text{II}$

3. $\frac{1}{2} = \exists - \text{II}$

4. $\frac{7}{12} = \wedge + \text{II}$

5. $1 = \text{II} + \exists$

6. $1 \frac{1}{12} = \exists + \wedge$

7. $\frac{1}{3} = \oplus - \Diamond$

8. $\frac{5}{12} = \exists - \wedge$

9. $1 \frac{1}{6} = \triangle + \oplus$

10. $\frac{1}{6} = \wedge - \Diamond$

84. MATCHING RATIOS TO FORM PROPORTIONS

1. H   2. C   3. J   4. E   5. G   6. B   7. A   8. F   9. D   10. I

85. USING RATIOS TO SAVE MONEY

1. a = $8.00 (better buy)   2. b = $40.00   3. b = $31.00   4. b = $4.00   5. a = $22.40
6. b = $18.00   7. b = $6.00   8. b = $39.00

86. 52 CARD PROBABILITY

1. $\frac{1}{52}$ 2. $\frac{1}{2}$ 3. $\frac{4}{50}$ or $\frac{1}{13}$ 4. $\frac{1}{2}$ 5. $\frac{8}{52}$ or $\frac{2}{13}$ 6. $\frac{39}{52}$ 7. $\frac{12}{52}$ or $\frac{3}{13}$

8. $\frac{52}{52}$ or 1   9. $\frac{10}{13}$ 10. $\frac{1}{52}$ 11. $\frac{1}{52}$ 12. 0   13. $\frac{16}{52}$ or $\frac{4}{13}$ 14. $\frac{1}{52}$